GETTING TO KNOW
THE U.S. PRESIDENTS

D0514633

T H O M A S
JEFFERSON

THIRD PRESIDENT
1801 – 1809

WRITTEN AND ILLUSTRATED BY MIKE VENEZIA

CHILDREN'S PRESS®
A DIVISION OF SCHOLASTIC INC.
NEW YORK   TORONTO   LONDON   AUCKLAND   SYDNEY
MEXICO CITY   NEW DELHI   HONG KONG
DANBURY, CONNECTICUT

Reading Consultant: Nanci R. Vargus, Ed.D., Assistant Professor, School of Education, University of Indianapolis

Historical Consultant: Marc J. Selverstone, Ph.D., Assistant Professor, Miller Center of Public Affairs, University of Virginia

Photographs © 2004:
Bridgeman Art Library International Ltd., London/New York: 16 (Blickling Hall, Norfolk, UK, National Trust Photographic Library/Christopher Hurst), 3, 25 right (New-York Historical Society, New York, USA)
Brown Brothers: 4
Corbis Images: 27 (AFP/Chicago Historical Society), 24 (Archivo Iconografico, S.A.), 9, 14, 30 (Bettmann), 11
North Wind Picture Archives: 28, 31 bottom, 31 top
Robertstock.com/R. Gilbert: 5
Steve Wolowina: 26
Superstock, Inc.: 20 (Stock Montage), 25 left (The Huntington Library, Art Collections, and Botanical Gardens, San Marino, CA), 19, 32

Colorist for illustrations: Dave Ludwig

Library of Congress Cataloging-in-Publication Data

Venezia, Mike.
  Thomas Jefferson / written and illustrated by Mike Venezia.
      p. cm.—(Getting to know the U.S. presidents)
Summary: An introduction to the life of Thomas Jefferson, a man whose
ideas helped create a new kind of government and who became the nation's
third president.
  ISBN 0-516-22608-8 (lib. bdg.)   0-516-27477-5 (pbk.)
  1. Jefferson, Thomas, 1743-1826—Juvenile literature. 2.
Presidents—United States—Biography—Juvenile literature. [1.
Jefferson, Thomas, 1743-1826. 2. Presidents.] I. Title.
  E332.79.V46 2004
  973.4'6'092–dc21

                              2003000009

16 17 18 19 R 18 17 16

A portrait of Thomas Jefferson by Rembrandt Peale (New-York Historical Society, New York)

Thomas Jefferson was the third president of the United States of America. He was born on his family's plantation in the colony of Virginia in 1743. Thomas Jefferson is best known for his intelligent and important ideas.

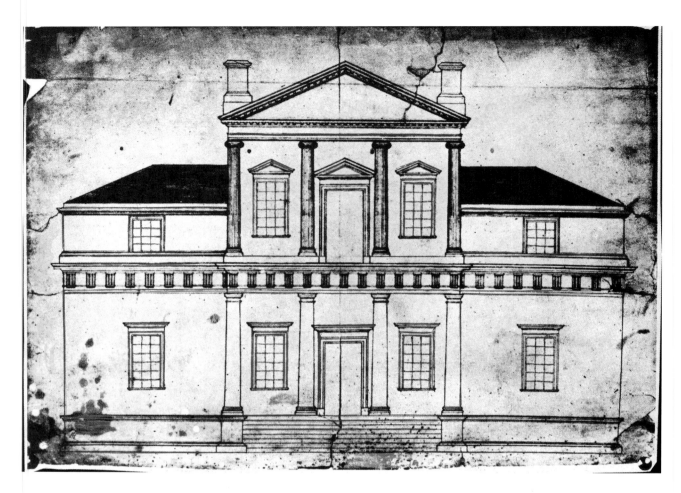

This is Thomas Jefferson's first drawing for the home he built at Monticello.

Thomas Jefferson believed ideas were the most powerful tools people could use. By thinking hard and coming up with good ideas, Thomas Jefferson invented ways to grow better fruits and vegetables on his plantation. He also designed a beautiful house all by himself.

Thomas built his house in an area he called Monticello, which in Italian means "little mountain." Everyone who saw Monticello admired it.

Most importantly, Thomas Jefferson's ideas helped create a new kind of government. This government cared about people's freedom and their right to do what they want with their lives.

Thomas Jefferson's home at Monticello

A government that cared about people's rights was unheard of during Thomas Jefferson's time. Throughout history, kings, queens, czars, and emperors had usually made the decisions about how people would live their lives.

When Thomas Jefferson was growing up, Virginia was a colony owned by England. The king of England at that time was George II. He got along pretty well with the people of the thirteen colonies in North America. It wasn't until later, when his grandson George III took over, that problems began.

The large plantation that Thomas Jefferson grew up on was called Shadwell. Most people who owned plantations had names for them. Thomas's father grew tobacco and other crops on his land. Mr. Jefferson was happy to teach his curious son all about farming. Thomas also learned how to build barns, stables, and storage sheds.

An engraving showing Cherokee leader Outacite

Thomas Jefferson was most interested in learning how to survey. He loved going out into the wilderness to map out and locate the boundaries of his family's land. Out in the wilderness, Thomas studied nature and met American Indians who lived in the woodsy areas that surrounded Shadwell. The Jeffersons sometimes invited Cherokee leader Outacite and some of his people to visit them.

The Jeffersons owned lots of land— and lots of slaves. In those days, plantation farmers depended on African slaves to clear the land, plow fields, and plant and harvest crops. No one thought much about slaves' rights in the 1700s. Plantation owners had been forcing black slaves to work on their plantations for years.

A cotton plantation in the South

Even though Thomas Jefferson owned slaves all his life, he knew it wasn't right. Thomas wrote a number of plans to stop or limit slavery. Slavery wasn't stopped, though, until years later, after the Civil War. Thomas Jefferson's ideas helped make the end of slavery finally possible.

When Thomas Jefferson was fourteen years old, his father died. Everyone was shocked because Mr. Jefferson had been known for his strength and energy. Being the oldest son in the family, Thomas inherited most of the plantation. At fourteen, he was suddenly very rich.

Thomas was ready to take charge of the plantation, but his mother told him that his father's last wish had been for Thomas to finish his schooling. Thomas followed his father's wishes. After finishing grade school, he entered William and Mary College in Williamsburg, Virginia.

Williamsburg was the capital of Virginia at the time. While at school there, Thomas attended parties where he met members of Virginia's government. Thomas became interested in how the government worked. He often went to government meetings and listened to important speakers there.

An engraving showing important buildings in Williamsburg in 1740

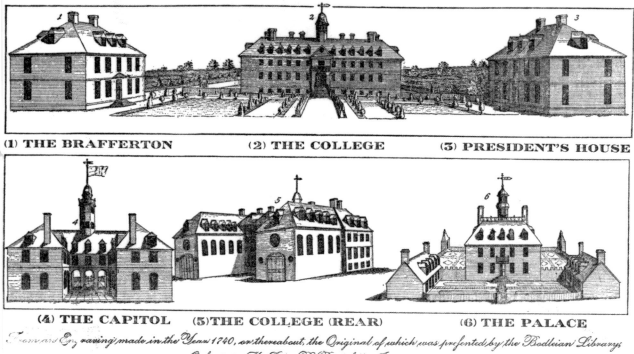

(1) THE BRAFFERTON (2) THE COLLEGE (3) PRESIDENT'S HOUSE

(4) THE CAPITOL (5)THE COLLEGE (REAR) (6) THE PALACE

From an Engraving made in the Year 1740, or thereabout, the Original of which was presented by the Bodleian Library, Oxford, to Mr. John D. Rockefeller, Jr., in 1937.

After he graduated from college, Thomas became a successful lawyer. He spent his spare time working on his new home at Monticello, adding rooms and trying out new architectural ideas. One night at a party, he met a girl named Martha Skelton. Martha and Thomas got along really well and ended up getting married in 1772. Even though Thomas's house wasn't finished, the newlywed couple moved in anyway.

As time went on, Thomas became more involved in the government of the Virginia Colony. He learned there were serious problems between the thirteen colonies and Great Britain. It seemed as if the king was always doing something to make people angry.

King George III made the colonists pay lots of extra taxes without giving them any say in

the matter. Once, when the colonists refused to pay taxes on tea, King George closed down Boston's harbor as a punishment. He then sent British soldiers to keep an eye on the colonists and make sure they behaved themselves.

A portrait of King George III of England by Allan Ramsay (Blickling Hall, Norfolk, England)

At one government meeting, Thomas heard the patriot Patrick Henry make a speech. Patrick was fed up with England and the king. He said he would rather die than be treated unfairly by England. Patrick Henry's fiery speeches made lots of colonists want to rebel against England. Thomas Jefferson and others agreed. In 1775, some battles broke out between the colonists and British soldiers, touching off the Revolutionary War.

In 1776, Thomas Jefferson traveled to Philadelphia, Pennsylvania. He joined leaders from other colonies there at a meeting called the Continental Congress. This meeting was set up to discuss what the colonies were going to do about King George and the British government. The leaders of the colonies decided to break away from England. They asked George Washington to head up their army, and chose Thomas Jefferson to write a Declaration of Independence.

This painting by J. L. G. Ferris shows Thomas Jefferson (at right) working on the Declaration of Independence with Benjamin Franklin (at left) and John Adams (center).

Thomas Jefferson ended up writing one of the most important historical documents ever. He wanted the declaration to make it absolutely clear why the colonies wanted to become their own nation. His beautifully written document is filled with ideas about rights and freedom for all people. On July 4, 1776, the Declaration of Independence was approved.

General Washington leading his soldiers during a Revolutionary War battle in 1777

As the Revolutionary War continued, Thomas Jefferson headed back to Virginia. In 1779, Thomas became the governor of Virginia. Even though it was a busy job, Thomas still found time to plant crops, work on his house, and read his favorite books.

While Thomas was governor, British soldiers attacked Virginia and caused a lot of damage. Thomas Jefferson was criticized for not spending enough time preparing for war and defending Virginia. Jefferson always felt he had let the people of Virginia down.

Finally, after six years of fighting, the Revolutionary War ended. The British gave up at Yorktown, Virginia, in 1781, and a peace treaty was signed in 1783.

After the war, Thomas Jefferson traveled to Paris, France, to join Benjamin Franklin and John Adams. These three patriots asked European countries for loans. They also worked out some business deals that would help the new United States of America.

Thomas enjoyed traveling all over Europe.
He learned as much as he could about architecture,
scientific discoveries, and new methods of
farming. While in Italy, Thomas learned about
a special type of rice. He thought this rice might
grow well in the United States, but the Italian
government said it would arrest anyone who
tried to take rice out of Italy. Thomas Jefferson
was so interested in the rice that he snuck some
out of Italy anyway by stuffing it in his pockets!

A portrait of George Washington (known as the Landsdowne portrait) by Gilbert Stuart (National Portrait Gallery, Smithsonian Institution, Washington, D.C.)

In 1789, George Washington became the first president of the United States of America. He asked Thomas Jefferson to be one of his closest advisors. Even though Thomas Jefferson was itching to get back to Monticello to spend time farming, reading, and writing about his latest ideas, he accepted the position of secretary of state.

A portrait of Thomas Jefferson by Charles Willson Peale (the Huntington Library, Art Collections and Botanical Gardens, San Marino, California)

A portrait of John Adams by Bass Otis (New-York Historical Society, New York)

Thomas still felt bad about the job he had done as governor of Virginia. He thought that maybe he could make up for it by helping his new country get off to a good start.

Thomas Jefferson did an excellent job. A few years later, he became John Adams' vice president. Then, in 1800, Thomas Jefferson was elected third president of the United States.

The Rocky Mountains today

Thomas Jefferson was president for two terms, which is eight years. One lucky thing that happened while he was president was that he got the chance to buy the Louisiana Territory. This gigantic piece of land stretched all the way from the Mississippi River to the Rocky Mountains. It included the important city of New Orleans.

An 1803 painting of the city and port of New Orleans by French artist
John L. Boqueta de Woiseri

Spain and then France had owned this territory. President Jefferson had been worried when France took it over. He knew that the French emperor, Napoleon Bonaparte, was interested in ruling the world. If Napoleon wanted to, he could cause a lot of problems for the new United States. For one thing, he controlled the busy shipping port of New Orleans.

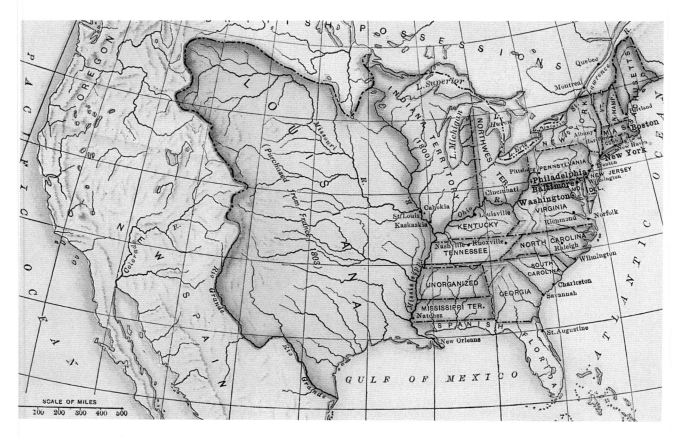

A map of the United States as it appeared in 1803

Thomas Jefferson decided to send a friend and advisor, James Monroe, to France to see if the United States might be able to buy New Orleans. James Monroe was surprised to discover that not only would Napoleon be happy to sell New Orleans, but he would throw in the whole Louisiana Territory for only $15 million.

Napoleon needed money right away to help pay for the wars his country was fighting. When Thomas Jefferson signed the agreement in 1803, he just about doubled the size of the United States.

An illustration showing Sacagawea, a Shoshone woman, guiding the Lewis and Clark Expedition through the Rocky Mountains

The Louisiana Territory was about 800,000 square miles (2,071,990 square kilometers) in size. There was a lot of unexplored land west of the Rocky Mountains, too. President Jefferson thought it would be a good idea to send someone to find out about the land that went all the way across North America to the Pacific Ocean.

These sketches from William Clark's diary show some of the wildlife Lewis and Clark saw during their expedition.

Jefferson asked Meriwether Lewis and William Clark to lead an expedition. In 1804, they headed west to explore unknown rivers and mountains.

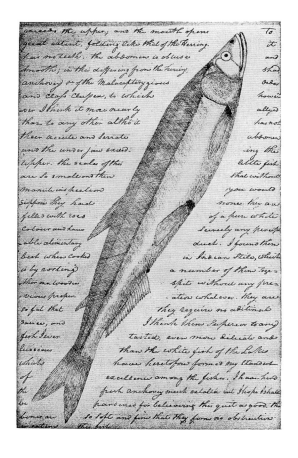

They were instructed to make friends with American Indians and learn about their customs. Lewis and Clark wrote lots of notes about the amazing things they saw.

A portrait of Thomas Jefferson at home at Monticello

Unfortunately, President Jefferson did have some problems he wasn't able to tackle. One of the biggest ones was that French and English navy ships began to stop American ships. They took cargo and kidnapped sailors for their own crew. Jefferson wasn't able to solve this problem and had to leave it for the next president to deal with.

When Thomas Jefferson finished his second term as president, he was happy to get back to Monticello. He spent his time coming up with important ideas about education and people's rights. He died on July 4, 1826, exactly fifty years after the Declaration of Independence was approved.

SS: THE SECRET ARCHIVES

WESTERN FRONT

WESTERN FRONT

IAN BAXTER

First edition for the United States, its territories
and dependencies, and Canada published in
2003 by Barron's Educational Series, Inc.

Copyright © 2003 Amber Books Ltd

All inquiries should be addressed to:
Barron's Educational Series, Inc.
250 Wireless Boulevard
Hauppauge, NY 11788
http://www.barronseduc.com

Library of Congress Catalog Card Number 2002117419

International Standard Book Number 0-7641-5674-8

Editorial and design by
Amber Books Ltd
Bradley's Close
74–77 White Lion Street
London N1 9PF
www.amberbooks.co.uk

Printed and bound in Italy by: Eurolitho S.p.A., Cesano Boscone (MI)

9 8 7 6 5 4 3 2 1

Picture Credits:

A special thankyou goes to Richard White and Martin Kaludow for providing
some of the photographs for this volume.

All other images in this book are credited to the HITM ARCHIVE.

www.militaria-net.co.uk/hitm.htm

This volume is dedicated to Michelle

CONTENTS

TRAINING FOR WAR

Following Germany's defeat in World War I, Adolf Hitler rose to become the leader of the newly-formed Nazi Party.

The *Sturmabteilung* (Storm Troops) or *SA* protected Party meetings. But after the abortive Munich putsch the *SA* and Nazi Party were banned. However, the ban did not deter Hitler's need for a new kind of bodyguard after his release from prison in 1924. Small groups were given the task in each Nazi *Gau* or region. In time, these local bodyguards were given the title as the *Schutz Staffel* (Protection Squad) or *SS*. These local shock troops quickly earned respect for their toughness and consolidated their role within the Nazi Party.

When Heinrich Himmler was appointed *Reichsführer-SS* in January 1929, the fate of the *SS* changed. The bespectacled former chicken farmer set out to create one of the most infamous organisations in military history. To Himmler, his *SS* were to become the elite of the German race. All prospective members were to be racially pure, physically fit and, above all, loyal and willing to sacrifice their own lives for Adolf Hitler.

LEFT: The first *SS* artillery regiment emerged in 1939 to serve with the *SS-Verfügungs* Division. The troops are training with the standard army 10.5cm (4.13in) leichte Feldhaubitze 18 (leFH 18) field howitzers.

By the early 1930s the *SS* had undoubtedly become the select body within the Nazi hierarchy. In 1934 it proved its worth in blood during the Röhm Purge, which saw the murder of many of the *SA* leaders. After the dramatic restoration of Hitler's power by purge, the *SA* were now a chastised unarmed body in existence as servants of the Party. With the *SA* emasculated, the *SS* now consolidated its power. Hitler quickly felt secure, and the building blocks of the armed branch of the *Schutz Staffel* began in earnest. Soon Hitler reconfirmed to Himmler his intention of raising a formation of armed *SS* soldiers that could prove their worth at the front in the same way as the army could make blood sacrifices on the battlefield. Almost immediately the *SS-Verfügungstruppe* (Special Disposal Troop) was formed. Eventually this newly-armed *SS* formation would create the basis of a full-scale *SS* fighting division. Although at first Hitler was less open about the use of this new *SS-Verfügungstruppe*, by 1935 he revealed that in time of war the *SS-VT* would be incorporated into the Army. Between 1933 and 1939, the power of the *SS* grew considerably with thousands of men being recruited into the new ideological elite armed formation under the command of Himmler.

All early recruits into the *SS* were expected to meet very stringent criteria. Each individual had to be tall, in the bloom of youth, and was required to have perfect eyesight. Furthermore, every new volunteer had to be fit with excellent racial features and produce a certificate of good behaviour from the police. Although the recruitment programme for the volunteers was difficult, the training was equally tough.

The initial training was carried out in various depots outside each *SS-VT* regiment's home town. The gruelling training programme was set-up by the Inspectorate of the *SS-VT*, *SS-Obergruppenführer* Paul Hausser. Hausser was one of the most influential commanders of the *SS*, and with the aid of two other experienced officers, *SS-Obergruppenführer* Felix Steiner and Caius Freiherr von Montigny, he rigorously trained the new recruits as assault troops, consisting of small groups of heavily armed volunteers. The recruit's day started at 0600 hours, with an hour's physical training prior to breakfast. The morning usually comprised of weapons training. Out on exercise they carried only weapons, ammunition, water bottles and field dressings, and were not weighed down with heavy packs, like their Army counter-

> ## Hitler created the SS. It was he who gave its members the notion that they were chosen men, ready to do whatever the *Führer* asked.

parts. Out on the rifle ranges they became used to their rifles. Once they were very familiar with their weapons they were taught infantry assault techniques that included charging at sandbags with bayonets fixed. Every *SS* instructor placed great emphasis on aggression and every possible means in which to overcome the enemy quickly and efficiently, with the least amount of friendly casualties. Unlike the Army, whose basic training was drill and more drill, *SS* training emphasized physical toughness and fighting skills.

To increase every candidate's aggressive spirit, boxing featured as a major part of the training, helping some of the men who needed to overcome the instinctive fear of being hurt. When the trainees were not boxing and enhancing their physical fitness and reflexes, they were in the classrooms learning how to strip, clean and reassemble their rifles. Their instructors, with the aid of a large wall chart, showed the weapons in exploded view, to explain thoroughly the function of each part. The men then had to practise on their own weapons, constantly repeating the disassembly and reassembly process until they could do it blindfolded. It was very important to become familiar with the weapons they were using and for this reason the recruits were literally drilled for hours on end. Every candidate was pushed to the limits of his endurance. They were constantly sent

ABOVE: These artillerymen have followed their training procedure to the letter. In the artillery service manuals the field artillery command stated: '...in order to be able to provide decisive action in infantry combat [the field artillery must] dispense with the advantages of concealed positions and provide its fire mostly from open positions....' In practice, this could be a recipe for disaster, and *SS* artillerymen paid a high price in

lives for this aggressive attitude. The white cap band and arm band worn by the artillery NCO on the right indicates that he is an exercise umpire. The other members of the gun crew are all wearing red-and-yellow battle-practice helmet bands. In training, military units were usually divided into two opposing sides and the battle-practice helmet band identifies which side a soldier was on.

on long foot marches with or without full kit, in order to develop stamina and endurance. Great emphasis too was placed on 'household' tasks. Mainly in the afternoon they pressed and repaired their uniforms and generally kept their barracks clean and tidy. The evenings were usually the recruits' own, when many of them relaxed, played cards or chess, read, listened to the radio and thought about loved ones.

At least three times a week the trainees had to endure formal lectures, covering policies of the Nazi Party, which included a very in-depth indoctrination in *SS* philosophy. The lecturers covered many topics and in particular the theories of racial superiority over what they regarded as 'subhuman Slavs and Jews'. These ideological lectures were aimed at producing men who ardently believed in the new Aryan order. Each one of them was indoctrinated into an almost fanatical determination to fight for the *Führer*, even if it meant shedding one's own blood on the battlefield.

Training for the men continued to be very intensive—so much in fact that it saw one recruit in three failing basic training the first time round. Those trainees successful enough to pass were rewarded with the passing-out parade, where the *SS* oath was taken. The candidate then had to spend a year in one of the *SS* infantry or cavalry schools, before returning to Munich to swear another oath of blind allegiance to Himmler. The *SS* recruit was now an ordained *SS* soldier. He was an elite warrior, highly mobile, whose training programme had been rigorous and fanatical. He had been dehumanized with an unswerving loyalty to Adolf Hitler. The consequences of his training and the indoctrination in *SS* philosophy made him a man who placed little value on his own life, and even less on his enemies'. With blind allegiance he was to step out and join one of the newly created armed *SS* divisions where he would obey every order, even if it meant shooting prisoners and committing atrocities against civilians.

ABOVE: This photograph was taken in August 1939 and shows an artillery battery on exercise. It is quite evident that howitzers out in the open were difficult to conceal. In the artillery training manual it was recognised that 'individual platoons or batteries of field artillery, with their guns and ammunition wagons, formed a very conspicuous target, prematurely betrayed troop concentrations for attack, and could be attacked on the battlefield by infantry weapons'. Thus artillerymen were trained to conceal their weapons, only moving into firing positions at the last moment. Artillery training was gruelling, but during the war, artillery firepower became a key player in offensive and defensive successes of the SS and the *Wehrmacht*.

LEFT: Two 10.5cm (4.13in) light field howitzers flank the Nazi War Ensign, as a cavalry school is prepared for a ceremonial parade. All SS *Verfügungstruppe* spent a year in one of the SS infantry or cavalry schools, before returning to Munich to swear a personal oath of allegiance to Adolf Hitler. Training emphasised toughness and comradeship producing SS men willing to sacrifice their lives for the *Führer*.

ABOVE: Training in August 1939, just prior to the invasion of Poland. Here *SS* artillerymen are moving their 10.5cm (4.13in) leichte Feldhaubitze 18 (leFH 18) light field howitzer into place. There were always hours of rigorous intensive artillery training where the artillerymen had to learn all aspects of their weapon, including learning from service manuals that contained detailed technical information and thorough instructions for handling the weapon. All gun crews were taught to aim the gun quickly and accurately, a prerequisite for fast and effective firing. The three-battalion *SS* motorised artillery regiments had 36 10.5cm light field howitzers on strength. In combat after September 1939 they came under Army command.

LEFT: *SS* artillerymen training with their guns, limbers and ammunition carriers. Just two months after this photo was taken these men would be in action in Poland advancing out of East Prussia towards Warsaw. Although the *SS* artillery batteries were relatively successful in Poland, the lack of heavy artillery meant that they had difficulty in destroying fortified enemy defences and conducting counter-battery fire.

RIGHT: A photograph taken at a training camp just prior to the attack on Poland in 1939. Surprisingly for the nation which invented *Blitzkrieg*, the German Army was still mainly horse-drawn at the outbreak of war. This was not a problem for the artillery, however, since most German infantrymen marched into battle on foot. Only the fast-moving Panzer divisions needed vehicle-towed or self-propelled artillery.

ABOVE: Dawn at a cavalry school in July 1939, as an *SS-Verfügungstruppe* artillery battery sets off on an exercise. Most German artillery was horse-drawn during the early years of the war. Once the gun had reached its firing position the crew unlimbered the horses, removed all the necessary items of equipment from the gun carrier and then placed the weapon into position. What made it even more difficult for the gun crews was that whenever the guns had to be moved the units had to keep and maintain their own stable of horses, and a good proportion of the supply capacity supporting any German unit had to be dedicated to horse fodder. Mobility across open country also posed a big problem, and in the Polish campaign artillery batteries had often been criticised for being unable to keep up with advancing infantry, let alone armour. This was as true of the newly formed *SS* Artillery Regiment and the artillery batteries attached to the three *SS-Verfügungstruppe Standarte* or regiments as it was of any Army unit.

BELOW: Gunners belonging to an unidentified *SS* artillery battery relaxing following intensive training prior to mobilization in June 1939. The artillery piece is a Rheinmetall-developed 10.5cm (4.13in) leichte Feldhaubitze 18 (leFH 18) light field howitzer that was the standard field piece found in the *SS* light batteries of the period. It was in June 1939 that the first troop movements to the east began, in preparation for the invasion of Poland. The first phase of mobilization was carried out between mid June and 15 July, when four infantry divisions moved to Pomerania and Silesia. Five more infantry divisions were dispatched between 15 July and 4 August. In some instances troop units dispatched to the frontier regions were returned to their home bases before arriving at their command areas, allaying Polish fears of an imminent German attack. This *SS* artillery battery was moved to East Prussia where it was attached to an Army infantry division. In the field assembly areas huge tented encampments were created, equipped with water points, field bakeries and bath facilities. The assembly areas were carefully camouflaged against reconnaissance from the air. Week by week convoys of men and equipment arrived daily, with trains and vehicles unloading new cargoes of tanks, artillery and shells. The vast business of marshalling German *Wehrmacht* and *SS* formations would continue up to and beyond the invasion date, set at that time for 26 August 1939.

ABOVE: Training for war. *SS* artillerymen pose for the camera prior to mobilization for the invasion of Poland. These gunners were soon to be moved to East Prussia where they joined the *Wehrmacht*'s 3rd Army. The 3rd Army included the 1st, 11th, 12th and 21st Infantry Divisions, together with the 217th Division, a cavalry brigade, an armoured and motorized division. The three *SS-Verfügungstruppe (SS-VT) Standarte* were dispersed, each operating seperately under Army Command, while the *SS* artillery regiment was under the command of Division *Kempf*. Men and units were to become increasingly familiar with this kind of 'shedding', not just for the Polish campaign, but also through other operations of its kind in the future. The *SS* regiments were not combined to form a single major *SS* fighting unit until the French campaign.

ABOVE: *SS* artillery crews rest following a gruelling exercise near Munsterlager in the summer of 1939. It was at Munsterlager that the *SS-Artillerie* Regiment was established. The *SS-Artillerie* Regiment was pronounced combat ready just two months prior to the invasion of Poland. The regiment itself was commanded by *SS-Obersturmbannführer* Peter Hansen.

Hansen, with the aid of training officers from the Army, hammered into his men that the main priorities of the artillery were the destruction of the enemy's anti-tank weapons, tanks, and artillery. However, in the early stages of the war the *SS* lacked the heavy long-range artillery needed to be truly effective in some of these roles.

ABOVE: A group of *SS* artillerymen use a rammer to clean the barrel of a 10.5cm (4.13in) light field howitzer during training prior to the invasion of Poland. The members of horse-drawn units such as this looked with envy on the few *Wehrmacht* mechanised artillery units, which used half tracks to tow their guns. Horses were slow, and it took a long time to move artillery pieces around the battlefield. Tracked vehicles towing light and heavy field howitzers not only allowed quicker and easier transport, but also had sufficient seating for the entire gun crew. With horses *SS* artillerymen frequently found it took them much longer to achieve fire readiness, and it also gave them a physically heavy workload.

LEFT: A heavily camouflaged howitzer seen during an exercise. Note the battle practice helmet bands. The red-and-yellow band was fixed by being buckled around the body of the helmet; three small metal hooks attached to the band by three short field-grey cloth straps hooked onto the rim of the helmet. All the men are wearing *Zeltbahn* or waterproof capes. When not in use the *Zeltbahn* was folded and worn strapped onto the wearer's field equipment. This type of single-colour waterproof cape was not used extensively by the SS during the war, being primarily a piece of *Wehrmacht* personal equipment. *SS Zeltbahn* were camouflaged, and despite serious shortages were issued right up until the end of the war. The most popular forms of SS waterproofs were made in two variations of 'plane tree' camouflage pattern. In action, the cape was secured by being buttoned together at the right and left front and between the legs, and tucking the sides under at the shoulders.

RIGHT: A camouflaged 10.5cm (4.13in) howitzer is being prepared for firing. In this photograph the battery officer can be seen supervising one of his crews. For each pair of guns under his command the battery officer was supported by the platoon leader or by a senior NCO, who repeated any commands out loud. The platoon leader or NCO ensured that the battery comman-der's commands were strictly and properly carried out and that the artillery crews maintained discipline whilst in action. Though most battery officers were young commissioned officers, experienced sergeants could also perform the role.

RIGHT: As was normal procedure, the artillerymen have draped foliage over the barrel to break up the shape of the gun and help conceal it whilst out in the open. Combat experience soon showed that artillery support was of decisive importance in the preparation and successful conduct of an attack. Artillery preparation before an attack was vital, and was intended to destroy, or at least to neutralise, the opponent's anti-tank defence in the area between the line of contact and the regimental reserve line, and to suppress enemy artillery fire. Each artilleryman was taught that continuous counter-battery fire prevented the enemy from shelling the tank assembly area and from breaking up the preparation of the tank attack.

ABOVE: Under supervision of an umpire, the crew of a 10.5cm (4.13in) howitzer fires its projectile under simulated battle conditions. *SS* training imbued all soldiers with high morale, aggression and a belief that they were a political and military elite. When not on the firing ranges or on exercise all recruits had to attend indoctrination classes. For hours the lecturers immersed the recruits in *SS* philosophy, particularly the theories of racial superiority over what they considered were 'subhuman' Slavs and Jews. Although most recruits listened to these seemingly interminable lectures, the majority, if not all of them, preferred testing their capabilities on the firing ranges, or undertaking long technical battle simulations.

LEFT: Smiling for the camera an artillery-man belonging to the *SS-Verfügungstruppe* holds an artillery shell destined for a 10.5cm (4.13in) light field howitzer. Note the specially designed wooden crates that were used to transport the shells safely. Soon these troops would have to transport their cargo of shells across some of Poland's roughest roads; virtually all Polish roads were sandy tracks. Excessive use made them virtually impassable, especially to horse-drawn gun crews towing cumbersome artillery pieces and heavy loads of artillery ammunition, not to mention fodder for the horses and food for the men. In the wake of the great armoured spearhead which drove across Poland, horse-drawn artillery and its horse-drawn supply chain was at times inevitably left behind. This lack of support would, in some places, cause the front to become overstretched. It was a problem that would be repeated on a much larger scale for both *Wehrmacht* and *Waffen-SS* artillery crews during the invasion of the Soviet Union in June 1941, with terrible consequences for Germany.

RIGHT: Marching from their barracks, an honour guard of the Armed *SS* follow the standard. To many *SS* men the *Feldzeichen* or Field Banner had an almost religious significance. Each banner was 'consecrated' by the Führer at the *Reichsparteitage* in Nuremberg, where it was brought into contact with the *Blutfahne*, the flag stained with the blood of Nazi 'martyrs' killed during the Munich Putsch in 1923. The Armed *SS* performed ceremonial duties from Hitler's seizure of power in 1933. On national or Party occasions these *SS* soldiers would march or stand vigil in their parade uniforms, complete with white belts, cross-straps, ammunition pouches and white gloves.

RIGHT: The third major armed *SS* formation was the *Totenkopf* Division. Formed around a core of members of the *Totenkopfverbände* or concentration camp guards, the division had little in common with the ferociously disciplined *Leibstandarte* or the *SS-VT*. Of the total of 15,000 men that made up the original *Totenkopf* Division, around 7,000 were from the pre-war *Totenkopfverbände*. Officers and men were often rotated between front line combat and guard duties in concentration camps. This became routine in many *SS* units through the war.

LEFT: During a brief respite from training three members of the *Totenkopfverbände* pose for the camera. Although nominally members of the Armed *SS*, the primary function of the *Totenkopfverbände* was to run the concentration camp system. Training of the *Totenkopf* guards took place at the unit's depot at Dachau. The training was very gruelling for the recruits and the day relatively long. The brutality found expression in the harsh and often murderous treatment of the camp's inmates. There was a considerable difference between the attitudes of the *Totenkopf* and the rest of the Armed *SS* – in many ways the camp guards were a brutal, undisciplined rabble whose character reflected that of its commander, a psychopathic killer named Theodore Eicke.

RIGHT: A *Totenkopf* recruit poses for the camera. The expansion of the *Waffen-SS* led to a shortage of uniforms with too few special *SS* tunics to go around. Instead, Army-issue tunics were distributed to the new *SS* divisions. From the French campaign onwards the wearing of standard army tunics became universal throughout the *SS* and remained the case until the end of the war. But what separated them from the standard uniforms worn by the *Wehrmacht* was the famous 'lightning flash' insignia denoting the *SS* on the collar. The other famous (or infamous) symbol was the *Totenkopf* or 'death's head'. Worn as a cap badge by all members of the *SS*, it replaced the 'Sig' runes on the collar patches of the *Totenkopf* Division, commemorating the unit's origins in the pre-war *Totenkopfverbände* or Death's Head camp guards. The basic *SS* rune collar patch became standard for all other *SS* soldiers during the war.

ABOVE: A group of *Totenkopfverbände* soldiers during training in 1939. They appear to be undertaking weapons cleaning. *Totenkopf* instructors put great emphasis on aggression and taught their recruits repeatedly techniques of unarmed combat. They also trained recruits on the art of bayonet fighting and taught them rigorously how to overcome enemy resistance quickly in order to minimise friendly casualties. Although this was no different from the way the

RIGHT: A group of soldiers pose for the camera at an *SS* barracks. *SS* training included a very strict physical programme, that was followed after breakfast with intensive weapons training. The men were then subjected to a couple of hours of target practice and unarmed combat training. After lunch they were given an intensive drill session, followed by cleaning the kit and then some more physical training on the sports field. Fitness and endurance were very important, the *SS* commanders requiring very high standards of their men. In fact, the physical training programme was so intense that the *SS* were usually much fitter than their *Wehrmacht* counterparts – it was all part of the image of a 'perfect Aryan' elite.

Wehrmacht trained its recruits, the real difference between the army and *SS* training was political indoctrination within the *SS* formations. This training was divided into three areas and the men had to sit in the classroom and be subjected daily to political training. They were taught the history of the NSDAP, the racial beliefs of the *SS*, and learnt carefully about the enemies of National Socialism. These enemies included the Jews, Freemasonry, Bolshevism and the church.

RIGHT: *Totenkopfverbände* soldiers pose for the camera during a pause in their gruelling training programme. The men of the *SS* learned about combat, underwent a strict physical training programme, and received political indoctrination. Perhaps the most important lesson that each one of them learnt was that they were part of a creed that looked after its own. Commanders strove at length to tell their men that they were part of a closed order with its own rules and regulations. They soon understood the meaning of obedience, honesty and dedication to duty. From the very first day they were recruited into the *SS* and put into training they were told that they were part of a military elite totally separate from the *Wehrmacht*.

BELOW: Training in the *SS*-style could be very hazardous, especially when the men were supplied with live ammunition during exercises. The training was meant to accustom individual soldiers to the conditions they would experience in battle. Such aggressive training led to inevitable fatalities, but the *SS* were firm believers in the 'train hard, fight easy' school. The training also made the average *SS* man much more willing to lay down his life in honour of *der Führer*. Here, one such live-fire training fatality is being buried with full military honours. The national flag has been draped over the coffin, and the soldier's M1935 steel helmet has been placed in the traditional style on top of the coffin as a mark of respect.

ABOVE: A group of *SS* troops are seen with their company commander during an exercise early in 1939. What made the Armed *SS* a particularly potent opponent in battle was its aggressive, no-holds-barred attitude towards fighting and the ardent belief of its men that they were invincible. They kept that attitude long after first being bloodied on the battlefield. For these men fighting was not, as it was for ordinary soldiers, simply a job, nor was their any conscript reluctance in the all-volunteer *SS*. For them, their blind faith in Adolf Hitler enabled them to go into combat armed with their fanatical allegiance to the *Führer* and with an ability to face the prospect of almost certain death that was unknown to most soldiers. As Himmler once said: 'Their lives are of value to them only as long as they can be used to serve the *Führer*'.

ABOVE: *SS* soldiers on a training exercise with a Horch
cross-country vehicle. Note the *SS* licence plate on the
rear of the Horch. The military-designed ideal to
create a perfect political fighting machine proved a
great attraction to the men that joined. They ardently
believed that stretching themselves both physically and
mentally marked them as true Nordic Germans, complete and proven men of Hitler's military elite. To these
idealists, the potent sacrificial spirit of the *SS* was able
to sustain them in the face of almost any adversary on
the battlefield.

RIGHT: A typical *SS* wardrobe displays hanging tunics
and two pairs of black boots. Aluminium mess tins
and other items of kit can also be seen. On top of the
wardrobe two M1935 steel helmets sit neatly on
pressed and folded kit, either side of two corrugated
gas mask holders. Although great emphasis was placed
on combat training and physical endurance, all *SS* men
were given daily cleaning and household tasks as well,
which included pressing and repairing of uniforms.
This type of activity was very similar to that of the
regular army, although the *SS* did not put as much
emphasis on the traditional Prussian 'spit and polish'.

ABOVE: An *SS* artillery battery on manoeuvres prior to the invasion of Poland. The crew for each individual gun was normally five or six men, and an experienced crew could keep up a rate of at least four rounds per minute. At intervals of two or three howitzers a battery officer would call out firing orders to the crews under his command, whilst one of the crew members checked the sight and called out the corrections required. Behind the 10.5cm (4.13in) light field howitzers a number of ammunition cradles can be seen. Prior to firing, the gunners would take the shells from the cradle and set the fuses ready for the next salvo. It was not unusual to see a large pile of primed shells laid out beside the gun.

BELOW: Before firing, the projectile had to be pushed into the barrel, followed by the cartridge case with a specified number of charges. Note the gas mask canister being worn by the crew. Pre-war gun crews trained to load and fire their artillery wearing gas masks – a skill which was not required during World War II. In a matter of weeks these troops were to see action in Poland, where they would learn that war was often harder than training. As part of the mixed Army and *SS* Panzer Division *Kempf*, they took three days to fight through the Polish defences at Mlawa. The difficulty was caused by the fact that the *SS* battalions had only light howitzers available and were unsupported by Ju 87 Stuka dive-bombers.

ABOVE: An interesting photograph at Münsterlager manoeuvre grounds shows *SS-Verfügungstruppe* moving their artillery and supplies out of their training camp during the summer of 1939. Some weeks earlier Hitler, accompanied by Himmler and various high-ranking *Wehrmacht* and *SS* officers, visited a combat exercise of the *Verfügungstruppe* at Münsterlager. The training operation featured a full-scale battle simulation by *SS* Regiment *Deutschland* and was supported by live ammunition barrages from *Wehrmacht* artillery batteries. The *SS* troopers, also using live ammunition, demonstrated their skilful assault tactics. Hitler was

very impressed with the demonstration, and as a result gave Himmler permission to establish the first fully-fledged *SS* division. Soon afterwards the *SS* was given equipment to begin the formation of an *SS* artillery regiment. However, as war approached the conversion of the *SS-Verfügungstruppe* into the *SS-Verfügungs* or *SS-VT* Division was temporarily postponed while its units, including a newly organised *SS-Artillerie* Regiment, were integrated into the *Wehrmacht* to prepare for action against Poland. The *SS* fought well, convincing Army sceptics who had doubted the quality of its training and equipment.

RIGHT: *Totenkopf* troops training in the snow early in 1939. It would not be until the winter of 1941 that these men would endure the hardships of combat in temperatures of 30 degrees below zero. It is clearly evident by their clothing that these men are not fully equipped to deal with winter warfare. The men are wearing the standard army tunics that remained universal throughout the *SS* during the war. However, they were supplemented with camouflage summer and winter smocks, sheepskin reversible clothing and two-piece white camouflage suits. In fact, by 1942 the *SS* were better clothed for combat than their *Wehrmacht* counterparts and were able to endure some of the bitterest weather conditions experienced in Russia for a century. The battle of the Demyansk Pocket in early 1942 was a prime example.

ABOVE: A *Totenkopf* detachment prepares for inspection. In spite of the view of the German High Command regarding the armed units of the *SS*, individual *Wehrmacht* commanders often had nothing but praise for their outstanding skill and endurance. Nevertheless a number of senior Army officers complained bitterly that their high casualty figures meant that the *SS* had not been trained properly for war. The figures partly reflected *SS* inexperience, and partly the fact that the *SS* was willing to accept higher casualties than the Army to achieve its goals.

LEFT: Four happy faced *SS* recruits smile for the camera during a pause in their training during the winter of 1939. According to Himmler, training was made as realistic as possible to ensure 'that every man became accustomed to his weapons and also to being within fifty–seventy metres of the explosion of his own artillery fire'. In the eyes of *SS* commanders it was imperative to use live ammunition in spite of the casualties, in line with the theory that 'every drop of blood in peacetime saved streams of blood in battle'. It was a combination of this tough, ruthless training and a willingness to fight to the death that made these men so effective on the battlefield.

RIGHT: A long column of troops belonging to the newly-formed *Totenkopf* Division seen on exercise in the early winter of 1939. The men are all wearing packs with rolled blankets. They are also wearing the standard army issue greatcoat but with *SS* insignia sewn onto the collars. It is interesting to note the uniformity of height. Initially, all applicants joining the *SS* had to be at least 178cm (5ft 10in) tall and of the highest physical fitness. Himmler insisted that the appearance of recruits should be purely Nordic; every *SS* man 'must be of well proportioned build; for instance there must be no disproportion between the lower leg and the thigh, or between the legs and the body; otherwise an exceptional bodily effort is required to carry out long marches. In his attitude to discipline the man should not behave like an underling, that his gait, his hands, everything, should correspond to the ideal which we set ourselves.' These recruiting qualifications reflected Himmler's 'Aryan' ideology and his desire to turn the *SS* into the foundation of a new, improved human race.

LEFT: A column of *Totenkopf* troops sets off on a march during a winter exercise near their training camp. Their commanding officer is on horseback and leads his men out through the German town. For these men, war would soon come. For their commanders it would be crucial that the *SS* should perform well in order to gain credibility on the battlefield as a military elite. They needed to be proven in battle. Time would undoubtedly prove these men to be products of one of the most efficient military training systems of World War II. As Himmler stated in 1939: '...It is only possible to perform this task if a part of the *SS* stands at the front and bleeds. Were we to bring no blood sacrifice and were not to fight at the front, we would lose the moral obligation to shoot people who sneak back home and are cowardly. That is the reason for the *SS-Verfügungstruppe*, which has the very noblest task, to be permitted to go into the field.'

ABOVE: Field kitchens are an important part of any military organisation. Keeping troops fed well in the field enables them to keep fighting effectively – hunger reduces combat efficiency remarkably quickly. This was particularly true in winter. *SS* field rations included rye bread, tinned meat or sausage, dried vegetables, jam or honey, coffee, sugar and cigarettes. This field kitchen is mounted on a railway truck, which is fine for exercises at home. However, it is much harder to feed an advancing army, and the *SS* soldiers also carried *Die Eiserne Portion* (iron rations) – tinned biscuits, tinned meat or leberwurst, and coffee (real or *ersatz*) – which provided sustenance for a day or two in emergencies.

RIGHT: An *SS* MG34 machine gunner and loader practicing with their potent weapon in the snow. In spite of the harsh weather conditions that these troops would experience on the Eastern Front the MG34 was a solid, rugged weapon and endured the harsh artic temperatures. The primary gunner – *Schütze* 1 – was perhaps the most experienced soldier in the MG squad. His team mate, *Schütze* 2, lying to the right of the gunner in the photograph, fed the ammunition belts and saw to it that the machine gun remained operational at all times. A typical MG squad consisted of a four-man crew with the two least experienced recruits bringing up fresh ammunition for the gun. Great emphasis was placed on the *SS* machine gunners finding the most advantageous defensive positions in order to halt an enemy advance.

BELOW: Out in the snow in early 1939 a commanding officer inspects the men of the *Totenkopf* Division. The period of enlistment in the original *Totenkopf-verbände* was initially four years. However, in 1938 this had trebled to 12 years. Before joining, all recruits had to go through a period of conscription in the armed services. Although this was intended to give them basic military training, not all the recruits were very happy undergoing another spell in military service once they had completed their national service requirement. It would not be until May 1939 that Hitler finally ordered that service with the *Totenkopf-verbände* would count towards the compulsory military requirement.

THE LOW COUNTRIES AND FRANCE

Prior to the Polish campaign in September 1939, the military units of Himmler's Armed *SS* had been untried in battle.

Following the Polish campaign, Hitler immediately turned his attention to a forthcoming campaign in the West, and decided to organise and expand the *SS* into a much larger fighting force. In late 1939 he agreed to the establishment of four new *SS* divisions. By March 1940 they became officially known as the *Leibstandarte*, an oversize regiment, and the newly formed *SS-Verfügungs*, *Totenkopf* and *SS-Polizei* Divisions.

By early May 1940 almost two and a half million soldiers allotted among 104 infantry divisions, 9 motorised divisions and 10 armoured divisions, had assembled their might along Germany's western borders from Switzerland to northern Holland. The divisions were organised

LEFT: Troops of the *Totenkopf* Division march westwards to the Belgian frontier on 12 May 1940. They waited for another four days before being committed to battle. They were assigned to Army Group A and were given plans to strike out across southern Holland, through Belgium and into France to link up with General Hoth's 15th *Panzer* Corps.

in three army groups. In the north Army Group B comprised two armies under the command of General von Bock. Army Group A consisted of four armies under General von Rundstedt, whilst Army Group C comprised two armies under the command of General Wilhelm von Leeb. Distributed among this huge army were the two SS formations *Leibstandarte* and the *SS-VT* Division. *Totenkopf* and the *SS-Polizei* Divisions were left in reserve.

During the night of 9/10 May 1940 the *Leibstandarte* and the *Der Führer* regiment of the *SS-VT* Division moved to their start lines with orders to link up with the airborne troops who would be dropped at dawn to seize vital bridges and airfields in the Low Countries. As day broke the *Leibstandarte* crashed into action across the Dutch border. The *Leibstandarte* raced 50 miles (80km) to its first objective, at Zwolle. The Dutch Army had demolished the bridge there, but the SS troops used barn doors as rafts to cross the River Ijssel.

At the same time, other SS formations were spearheading the advance through enemy territory. *Der Führer* drove at break-neck speed near Arnhem and became embroiled in heavy fighting for the Grebbe Line, whilst the remainder of the *SS-VT* Division fought its way through towards Moerdijk, where *Fallschirmjäger* had seized the bridge. On 11 May a French column reached Tilburg and later that day ran head on into half the 9th *Panzer* Division and the *SS-VT* Division. The French forces desperately tried to escape from the Panzers and motorised SS infantry. The French troops were driven back to Breda in disarray.

Over the next few days SS soldiers, along with their *Wehrmacht* counterparts, steamrollered through Holland. Outside the city of Rotterdam the *Leibstandarte* was preparing its attack positions for the assault into the Dutch capital. Following a heavy aerial bombardment of the city that killed 800 civilians and made 78,000 homeless, the *Leibstandarte* moved in. Within two hours the Dutch accepted the German terms of surrender. However, Sepp Dietrich's *Leibstandarte* carried on fighting, unaware of the surrender terms. Firing on a group of Dutch officers, they wounded the commander of Germany's *Fallschirmjäger* corps, *Generalmajor* Kurt Student.

The next day the *Leibstandarte* arrived at The Hague, but by this time the Dutch Army had finally surrendered. With the war in Holland over the *Leibstandarte* made a quick victory march north to Amsterdam, where it then turned south to take part in the French campaign.

By the time the Dutch surrendered the German offensive into Belgium and France was in full swing and the British, French and Belgian troops were in full retreat. The *SS-Totenkopf* Division was pulled out of reserve and ordered to exploit the enemies' deteriorating situation. Through Namur-Charleville, the division smashed its way through Belgium, joining up with advanced elements of the 5th and 7th *Panzer* Divisions. Although the SS troops fought hard, the division suffered its first casualties of the war: 53 wounded and 16 dead during the period 19–20 May.

'It will be your honour that you, the *Leibstandarte* which bears my name, will lead every attack'.

Adolf Hitler, 1940

During the evening of 20 May, the Germans finally reached the Channel coast west of Abbeville, at the mouth of the Somme. More than 40 French, British and Belgian divisions – some one million soldiers – were cut off from the main body of the French Army in the south. Over the next few days the Allied forces tried desperately to attack across the German salient in order to re-establish a front with the main French forces in the south. Although only a limited action by the Allies was launched at Arras, its effects totally surprised the 7th *Panzer* and the *Totenkopf* Divisions. What ensued was a vicious battle against the flanks of the mighty 7th *Panzer* and an elite SS division. Before the attackers were finally halted, they had thrown the *Panzertruppen* and *Totenkopf* Division into

LEFT: Passing destroyed vehicles of the French Army *Totenkopf* soldiers move on north and east of Cambrai. Although the *Totenkopf* had incurred its first wartime combat losses, with 16 dead and 53 wounded, it had in fact relieved the pressure on Rommel's 7th *Panzer* Division and allowed General Hoth's 15th *Panzer* Corps to continue its rapid advance through France. It was here along these dusty French roads that the *Totenkopf* became stuck in huge traffic jams in the area around Cambrai and Artois. Soon though, the *Totenkopf* were yet again in action supporting General Rudolf Schmidt's 39th Corps between the 8th *Panzer* Division in the south and the 7th *Panzer* Division in the north.

total disarray, leaving behind a trail of death and devastation.

Meanwhile on the Aa Canal, the 1st *Panzer* Division, to which the *Leibstandarte* were now attached, had compressed the Allied armies retreating towards the port of Dunkirk. The 3rd Battalion of the *Leibstandarte* was then ordered on 24 May to capture a 42m (138ft) hill, the Wattenberg, lying east of the canal. Shortly before the attack was due came the infamous *Führer* order to halt the tanks and stand fast. Nevertheless, the regimental commander, *SS-Obergruppenführer* Sepp Dietrich, chose to ignore Hitler's order. The *Leibstandarte* continued to push forward towards Watten until fierce British Expeditionary Force (BEF) resistance at Bollezelle halted it.

On the night of 26 May, Hitler rescinded his famous 'halt order' and the *Germania* and *Der Führer* Regiments of the *SS-VT* Division surged back into action and fought a bloody battle in the de-Nieppe forest. The remaining infantry regiment, *Deutschland*, which was temporarily attached to the 3rd *Panzer* Division, took part in the attack against British units on the Lys Canal near Merville where the *SS* troops met spirited resistance.

With the first phase of the war in the West completed, the Battle of France began. On 5 June 1940 German Panzer groups attacked along the whole line. As elements of *Panzergruppe Kleist* steamrollered towards Paris, *Leibstandarte* and the *SS-VT* Division joined the main drive. The *SS-Totenkopf* Division moved from Boulogne to St Pol, and kept there on alert. On 9/10 June, the horse-drawn *Polizei* Division was finally permitted to engage in an offensive operation of its own. During the crossing of the Aisne River and the Ardennes Canal the division became viciously embroiled against determined French units.

By the time the *SS* formations arrived on the outskirts of Paris the French capital had been abandoned by its government. *Panzergruppe Kleist*, including the *Leibstandarte*, *Totenkopf* Division, and *Verfügungs* Division, struck through Champagne toward Dijon in Burgundy to prevent the remnants of the French Army retreating to the south-west of France.

On 25 June 1940, the day on which the ceasefire went into effect, the *Totenkopf* and *Verfügungs* Divisions were near Bordeaux, preparing to occupy the coastal sector. The *Leibstandarte*, meanwhile, were south of the new demarcation line, near St Etienne, preparing to move north to Paris to take part in the victory parade. The *Polizei* Division was in reserve along the upper Maas near Rondilly.

For the *SS* the campaign in the West was over. Hitler declared: 'As a result of this war, the German Armoured Corps has inscribed for itself a place in the history of the world; the men of the *Waffen-SS* have a share in this honour.' Following Hitler's speech, the term *Waffen-SS*, or Armed *SS*, became the accepted designation for the field formations of this elite corps of men.

ABOVE: Soldiers belonging to the 4th *SS-Polizei* Division resting inside a ruined French town in June 1940. Although formed under the authority of *Reichsführer-SS* Heinrich Himmler the *Polizei* Division was not technically an *SS* division at this time. Prevented by the Army from recruiting soldiers from the general population, Himmler did however have a source of manpower in the police, which he controlled, and the division was made up from members of the *Ordnungspolizei*, the police force. Unlike the other *SS* divisions, this division was second rate and was not fully motorised. Instead of standard *SS* equipment the *Polizei* Division was equipped with old and captured hardware. When it was released for action in France the division was untried in battle. Its members were considerably older than other *SS* men, and their lack of training and poor equipment did not help to inspire the confidence of their *Wehrmacht* counterparts either.

LEFT: Men of the 1st Infantry Regiment, commanded by *Standartenführer* Max Simon, are seen here with captured Moroccan troops. This *Totenkopf* regiment had crossed the Sambre River and advanced towards Le Cateaux and Cambrai. They were in fact the first *Totenkopf* troops to enter the combat area and fought a series of bitter house-to-house battles with Moroccan forces. French units then counterattacked with tanks, but the *Totenkopf* infantry resisted fiercely and repelled a number of armoured strikes. It should be noted that the first day's fighting against the Moroccan units only saw about 100 of them captured. Most surrendering Africans were simply shot out of hand, being considered 'sub-humans'. The *Totenkopf* were the worst offenders, but all of the front-line *SS* divisions committed similar atrocities.

RIGHT: Troops of the 1st *Totenkopf* Infantry Regiment with a handful of captured Moroccan soldiers in the Cambrai region of France. By the end of the morning of 20 May 1940, *Totenkopf* units had successfully cleared the areas to the north and east of Cambrai and captured some 16,000 prisoners and a large amount of battle-field booty. During the fierce battle that saw the regiment incur the first combat casualties of the war, they claimed they had killed some 200 Moroccan soldiers with 100 survivors of the battle finally capitulating. It is uncertain just how many of the 200 Moroccan soldiers were executed, but it is clear that a high percentage of them were killed by racially motivated *Totenkopf* troops. During the next few days *Totenkopf* units re-established contact with French formations and took part in plugging the gaps left by the rapidity of the German armoured advance.

LEFT: A group of *Totenkopf* troops pose for the camera around an *SS* motorcycle combination in the Arras sector. It was in this area on 21 May 1940 that the *Totenkopf* Division sustained a heavy mauling by both British and French forces. However, the 7th *Panzer* Division fared considerably worse, losing 20 tanks and as many anti-tank guns. In spite of sustaining heavy losses the *Totenkopf* resumed its advance and pushed forward towards the town of Bethune, along the banks of the La Bassée Canal. This was a natural defensive barrier and when the *Totenkopf* entered the town to cross the canal it was met by a spirited British defence and was forced to retreat. It was not until 24 May that parts of the 3rd Infantry Regiment led personally by Theodor Eicke finally crossed downstream and established a bridgehead.

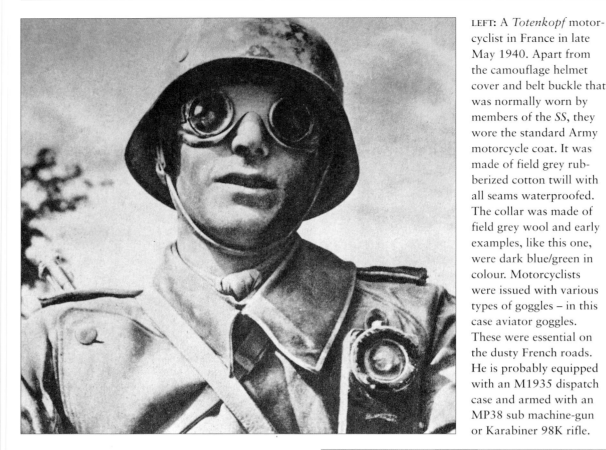

LEFT: A *Totenkopf* motorcyclist in France in late May 1940. Apart from the camouflage helmet cover and belt buckle that was normally worn by members of the *SS*, they wore the standard Army motorcycle coat. It was made of field grey rubberized cotton twill with all seams waterproofed. The collar was made of field grey wool and early examples, like this one, were dark blue/green in colour. Motorcyclists were issued with various types of goggles – in this case aviator goggles. These were essential on the dusty French roads. He is probably equipped with an M1935 dispatch case and armed with an MP38 sub machine-gun or Karabiner 98K rifle.

RIGHT: Theodor Eicke was the creator of the Nazi concentration camp system and of the *Totenkopfverbände* who ran it. When the *Totenkopf* Division was formed in October 1939, he was a natural choice as its commander. Eicke was a brutal thug, who hated the *Wehrmacht* and despised other *SS* units. But despite his arrogant and contemptuous nature, he was a gifted commander, idolised by his men. He was looked upon as a great organiser, and his determination infused the *Totenkopf's* military training, creating an aggressive and hard-charging unit on the battlefield. Eicke was disgusted when he was told that his cherished *Totenkopf* were to be held in reserve along with the second rate *Polizei* Division for the invasion of the Low Countries and France. When the *Totenkopf* were finally released from reserve on 16 May 1940 Eicke was determined to show the other *SS* and *Wehrmacht* units what his men were made of. They fought hard, but were also guilty of a number of atrocities.

RIGHT: Following the surprise halt order on 26 May 1940, detachments of *Totenkopf* infantry had nothing else to do than watch from the roadside endless fleeing refugees pouring westward through France not far from the La Bassée Canal. One of the biggest problems faced by *Waffen-SS* and *Wehrmacht* units during its drive through France was the number of refugees jamming the already congested roads. The British and French forces experienced the same problem, with the added complication of being subject to constant ground and aerial attacks as they withdrew ahead of the rapidly moving German armoured spearheads.

LEFT: *Totenkopf* troops being led by their commanding officer in front of intrigued German spectators. In December 1939 the *Totenkopf* Division was ordered to Ludwigsberg, just north of Stuggart, and placed in the second-line reserve for the attack in the West. Much to Eicke's dismay his men were initially relegated to occupation duties, while the *SS-Verfügungs* Division and *Leibstandarte* were unleashed in the first wave of attacks.

ABOVE: A *Totenkopf* machine gun team lays down fire from their MG34, which is mounted on a MG *Lafette* 34 tripod. These men are attached to Götze's 3rd Infantry Regiment. It was this regiment, supported by tanks of the 4th *Panzer* Division, that overwhelmed British positions around Locon on 27 May. Fighting in this area was particularly fierce but the *Totenkopf's* training and indoctrination prior to the French cam-

RIGHT: A well concealed *Totenkopf* position seen near Boulogne. The division had been temporarily pulled out of the line late in May 1940, and for a time it was deployed around the French town. The British commander in the Channel port, Brigadier William Fox-Pitt, had been given orders to defend the town to the last man and last round. While he hurriedly organised a defence in the hills which surrounded the port, British troops, under a storm of heavy concentrated fire, were being dramatically evacuated from the port by British warships. As German troops closed in to secure the port, remaining British soldiers tried to rush one of the last ships to leave the harbour. When the town fell on 25 May, *Panzergruppe Kleist* claimed to have taken over 2,000 prisoners. Many had been captured as they tried to fight their way out.

paign had imbued every *SS* soldier with a recklessness and determination which came to the fore whenever it carried out an attack. There is little doubt that these soldiers displayed considerable bravery, although they took many risks and suffered disastrous casualties as a result. *Wehrmacht* generals considered Theodor Eicke, the divisional commander, to be little more than a butcher – but he generally got results in battle.

ABOVE: A *Totenkopf* Division gunner in a forward observation post uses an optical range finder to correct fire for an artillery battery. Should rounds fall short or over the target, his task was to advise on the corrections needed to hit the target. An observation post would necessarily be within sight of the target to give accurate ranging information, which is why the soldier is concealed in long grass. This particular *SS* man is equipped with a camouflage smock and helmet cover that helps him blend well with the natural surroundings. The camouflage smock was the most innovative *SS* contribution to military uniforms during the war and as a result almost all modern soldiers wear various types of camouflage clothing when in the field.

LEFT: *Totenkopf* troops seen during a lull in the fighting in France. Note that these soldiers are wearing army issue tunics. This was due to the fact that following the expansion of the new *SS* divisions in 1939 there were not enough special *SS* tunics to go round. Consequently the troops wore a mixture of dress until after the French campaign, when the wearing of the standard army tunics became universal throughout the *SS*. Note the *Totenkopf's* special collar patches displaying the distinctive death's head. The two soldiers at the front of the photograph are both wearing standard equipment for a rifleman, including belt and cartridge pouches for the Kar 98K rifle. They also have M24 'stick' grenades pushed through their belt for ease of carriage. The soldier on the left is wearing a gas cape bag. This was the proper way of wearing the bag, but sometimes soldiers slung them around their backs instead of across the front of the chest.

BELOW: An infantry truck carrying *Totenkopf* troops is seen during the division's southward push to participate in the final defeat of the French Army. Foliage has been applied to the vehicle in order to help conceal it from the air. Rolled netting can also be seen, which was used when the vehicle was stationary for any length of time. Note the national flag draped over the engine deck for aerial recognition. Both *Waffen-SS* and

Wehrmacht units made extensive use of the red, white and black flag to avoid being hit by friendly fire, at least until 1943, when it was realized that the flag made them easy targets for the growing might of Allied airpower. By 1944, with the *Luftwaffe* almost swept from the skies, the *SS* rarely used flags on vehicles for aerial recognition, preferring to raise a flag in the air once they had identified friendly aircraft.

LEFT: *Totenkopf* vehicles move along a road during the division's drive south. *SS* infantry can be seen in the field next to an abandoned French Renault R-35 light tank. Of the 3,132 modern tanks available to the French forces in May 1940, some 900 were Renault R-35s. The R-35 was a light tank of 10 tonnes. Armed with a 3.7cm (1.45in) gun, it equipped 20 of the French Army's tank battalions. However, despite the number of modern armoured vehicles in the French inventory, they were used according to outdated doctrines. Unlike the French, the Germans realised that it was how a tank was used which made the difference. They made use of the tank's mobility, supported by well-coordinated air support, to run rings around the Allies.

RIGHT: A *Totenkopf* flak crew mans a 2cm (0.78in) *Flak-vierling* 38 quadruple-barrelled self-propelled anti-aircraft gun, which is mounted on the back of a halftrack artillery tractor. Following the Polish campaign the newly created *SS-Verfügungs* Division raised a three company light anti-aircraft battalion, each company being equipped with twelve of the quadruple mounts, which were mounted on Sd.Kfz.10 halftracks. The flak gun fired 0.12kg (0.26lb) high explosive, incendiary or armour-piercing rounds, and was capable of firing an impressive 450 rounds per minute from each of the four barrels. The flak crew wear camouflage smocks, but no helmet covers. Netting has been attached to the steel helmet instead, in order to hold foliage or grass in place. This method was used to varying degrees, and had the desired effect of breaking up the sharp outline of the helmet surface and making a hidden soldier even harder to see.

ABOVE: A well concealed *Totenkopf* 3.7cm (1.45in) Pak35/36 anti-tank gun overlooks enemy positions near Arras on 21 May 1940. At the time the *SS* possessed three companies of 12 3.7cm Pak 35/36s. In addition, the *Totenkopf* motorised reconnaissance battalion created a towed anti-tank platoon equipped with a further three guns. By the time the invasion had been unleashed the *Totenkopf*, together with the rest of the combined divisions of the *SS*, had a front-line strength of 90 Pak 35/36s – the first anti-tank gun to be used by the *SS*. The gun weighed 432kg (952.5lb) and had a sloping splinter shield. It fired a solid-shot round at a muzzle velocity of 762m/s (2,500ft/s) to a range of 4,025m (4,400yds). The gun was reasonably successful in Poland, but could not penetrate the thick armour of French Char B and British Matilda tanks.

RIGHT: *Totenkopf* men relax in a field in front of a World War I monument. By 14 June, the British had been forced off the continent and organised French resistance on the battlefield was quickly collapsing, while a large part of the French Army was still trapped in the Maginot Line. The *Totenkopf* joined the other *SS* divisions in the pursuit of what was left of the French Army. By this period of the campaign only French troops managed to surrender. French colonial forces still tried to resist, since they knew that they had no chance of survival, even if they capitulated. The *SS* considered them racial inferiors and shot them out of hand. Essentially, the drive south through France was one massive mopping-up operation for the men of the *Totenkopf* Division.

BELOW: Vehicles belonging to a *Totenkopf* Division unit have halted inside a French town. By the appearance of the faces of the troops they are in an ebullient mood, probably with news that the campaign in France is drawing to a victorious conclusion. According to the *Totenkopf* war diary, between 17 and 19 June 1940, the division had taken some 6,088 prisoners at a cost of just five dead and 13 wounded. The French campaign had undoubtedly proved the credibil-ity of the *Totenkopf*. The division had shown courage and resilience in combat, in spite of the poor leader-ship of its commanders that was mainly due to their inexperience. However, at the same time some of the units of the division had also shown its propensity for brutality. The killing of Moroccan soldiers and the massacre of British prisoners convinced their enemies that the *Waffen-SS* were a group of murderous fanat-ics, determined to destroy anything that resisted them.

LEFT: Two *Totenkopf* soldiers stand guard in front of a grave of their fallen *Waffen-SS* commander. Behind them are draped three flags that dwarf both the men. One flag displays the *SS* rune, and this is flanked by two national flags. This photograph was taken following a funeral ceremony. As with all *SS* funerals holding rank of officer, it was ritual for *SS* soldiers to stand guard over their fallen. Although always saddened by the loss of their leaders or comrades, each soldier was aware that he had been bound by his oath of loyalty to their *Führer* and had promised him obedience unto death.

ABOVE: Totenkopf engineers wearing *Waffen-SS* camouflage summer smocks construct a makeshift wooden bridge during the drive south. The battle of France was the kind of fighting that every *SS* soldier liked best, demanding improvisation, daring and, above all, speed. All through the campaign, the strategic impetus behind the advance was provided by armour. Time after time, the last remnants of the battered French Army operating in open country were checked or even forced to withdraw by boldly handled pockets of German armour and small groups of well-armed *SS* soldiers. It was quite evident, even during the opening phases of the battle of France, that the French Army, from the Marshals down to the ordinary *poilu*, could not match the superior fighting performance of its opponents on the battlefield. Yet for all the skill and toughness with which German operations were carried out, there were areas where advancing tank units were unable to make their familiar sweeps across open country due to isolated pockets of French resistance.

ABOVE: A group of *Totenkopf* soldiers pose for the camera following the defeat of the French Army in late June 1940. In spite of the success achieved by the *Totenkopf*, casualties had been considerably higher than initially expected. In fact, there were some 1,152, more than 10 percent of the unit's combat strength, killed in the battle for France. This high casualty rate was the product of not only feats of daring élan and courage under fire, but also due to the fact that *Totenkopf* officers were inexperienced, which consequently led many of the units to take unnecessary risks on the front lines. Previously sceptical *Wehrmacht* officers had to acknowledge *SS* bravery, but few had any time for their many acts of barbarism.

RIGHT: Members of the *Totenkopf* signals battalion operate their radio set in northern France. This was probably a forward observation post, from where information on target coordinates of routes for attacking armoured units was sent to higher commanders. Most *Waffen-SS* combat troops in 1940 were issued with camouflaged smocks. These were waterproof and were reversible. Various shades of camouflage were printed on either side of the smock. One side was predominantly green for spring and summer, the other brown for autumn and winter. Although the patterns varied, the combination of leaf shapes and spots was characteristic of all the smocks worn by the *SS*.

LEFT TOP: Troops attached to the horse-drawn *Polizei* Division in France. Even in 1940, the German armed forces depended on the horse for over 75 percent of their logistics. The mass of *Wehrmacht* and *SS* that followed in the wake of the handful of armoured divisions moved either on foot or by plodding horse. Although Hitler had every intention of making his army an all-mechanised force, when war broke out in September 1939 the majority of the divisions were still horse-drawn. The reliance of the German war machine upon horses is best appreciated by the fact that in 1940 on the Western Front more than 100,000 of them served in the opening phases of the campaign – even larger numbers were to be used in Russia a year later. The horses were used all through the *Wehrmacht* and SS, where they transported ammunition and supplies and towed artillery. Cavalry units were also deployed on the Western Front, where they were primarily used for security and reconnaissance.

LEFT BOTTOM: Soldiers belonging to the *Polizei* Division pause during their drive through France in June 1940. The *Polizei* Division used a variety of insignia. Police rank badges were used, and would continue to be used well into the war. Their uniforms too consisted of a mixture of army and SS, and their equipment was relatively antiquated compared to that of premier SS formations like the *Leibstandarte*. Initially the *Polizei* had been kept in reserve for the French campaign, being based at Tübingen behind the Upper Rhine front of Army Group C. Although the division did not see extensive action in France it none the less fought relatively well against spirited enemy resistance as it forced a crossing of the Aisne.

RIGHT: A group of motorcyclists from an unidentified *Totenkopf* regiment pause for a much-needed rest during its gruelling advance through France in early June 1940. They are all wearing the standard double-breasted rubberized motorcycle coat. When in use, the motorcycle waterproof coat was worn with army canvas and leather issue gloves or cloth mittens, with overshoes and leggings or just with normal boots. Three of the motorcyclists are wearing the M35/40 steel helmet with slate grey paint finish applied. Note the distinctive *SS* shield painted on the left side of the steel helmet. In the field the realities of combat in France led to many *SS* soldiers dulling their helmets by daubing them with mud. Soldiers found that getting rid of the shiny surface of the helmet reduced the risk of detection whilst under cover. The *SS* runes and National Party decals were also smeared and concealed with mud.

LEFT: Two *Totenkopf* soldiers consult a map on top of an Sd.Kfz.221 light armoured car near the La Bassée Canal. It was near here that frustrated *Totenkopf* troops, who had suffered heavy casualties against stiff British opposition, were ordered to murder 97 men of the Royal Norfolk Regiment who had been taken prisoner. The British soldiers had been surrounded in a farmhouse near the village of Le Paradis. They eventually ran out of ammunition and reluctantly marched out under a white flag to surrender to the 14th Company of *Totenkopf's* 1st Battalion of the 2nd Regiment. SS-*Obersturmführer* Fritz Knöchlein, the senior officer present, ordered the British prisoners to be led across a nearby road and into a barnyard, where they were subsequently machine-gunned in cold blood.

ABOVE: Soldiers from the 4th *SS-Polizei* Division have removed a horse-drawn cart from the main road, and are in the process of unloading its contents. Of particular interest are the two radio operators that appear to be either transmitting or receiving radio messages. They are both wearing earphones over their M1938 *Feldmütze*. All of the *SS* soldiers are wearing the German Army M1936. Their M1935 helmets are displaying the *Wehrmacht*-style eagle-and-swastika insignia. All of the men are wearing black leather marching boots. The men's personal kit is standard army issue, including a gas mask canister, rolled *Zeltbahn*, bread bag, mess tin, entrenching tool, bayonet and the usual belt and Kar 98K pouches.

RIGHT: A Pz.Kpfw.III armed with a 3.7cm (1.45in) gun acting in support of an advancing unit of the *Polizei* Division. When *SS* units attacked, they did so in small formations covered by their own heavy weapons and tanks, staying away from individual tanks because they drew the strongest enemy fire. When a tank company attacked with the infantry, there were normally two platoons on the line, one platoon back, and the fourth platoon in reserve. By the time the *Polizei* Division was released for action in June 1940 the need for armoured support slowly reduced as the Panzers achieved one victory after another. Some armoured units found themselves up to 24km (15 miles) ahead of the infantry, seldom encountering the enemy.

LEFT: A grave of two fallen *SS* soldiers belonging to the *Polizei* Division. *SS* runes have been white-washed into the freshly dug earth. This type of burial was common, especially for officers and NCOs. Much was made of *SS* troops killed in action, and funerals were tailored to suit Nazi ideology, particularly Himmler's notions about the fallen warrior of the Aryan–Nordic race. To the *Reichsführer*, the *SS* soldier was an exemplar of the new Aryan man, and if this 'warrior' was to be sacrificed on the battlefield, he was to be honoured at his funeral as a hero of the 'Black Order'. *SS* funerals were almost mystical occasions, which bound the individual who attended these ceremonies to believe that he was not only racially superior, but also part of an elite band of soldiers unified in one common cause – a fanatical determination to fight for the *Führer*, even if it meant shedding one's own blood on the battlefield.

RIGHT: The grave of a twenty-six-year-old soldier called Karl Koch who was attached to the 8th *Polizei* Rifle Regiment 1 of the *Polizei* Division. He was killed in France on 10 June 1940, just three days before the German Army's triumphant entry into Paris. During operations in France, the *SS* constantly showed its courage in the face of determined resistance, but at a heavy cost in blood. The *Polizei* Division, regarded as a second-rate unit, suffered particularly heavy casualties in France as a result of its quality in soldiery and equipment. During its brief deployment on the Western Front, units of the *Polizei* Division often found advances to be hard going, and they fought a series of hand-to-hand battles in an all-out effort to overcome the isolated French units who were putting up such stiff opposition.

ABOVE: Troops of the *Leibstandarte SS Adolf Hitler* cross a destroyed bridge over the River Marne on 12 June 1940. The Marne was reached by the 2nd Battalion of the *Leibstandarte*, which forced a crossing near St Avige. By that same evening the battalion cut the main railway line and later that night the regiment was taken out of line. During this period *SS* soldiers saw that the war on the Western Front had taken on the character of a battle of pursuit. It was fast becoming clear that the Western Allies now lacked the ability

to halt the German advance. The motorised *Leibstandarte* continued its furious drive, while slower divisions in the rear carried out the mopping-up operations. By 21 June the *Leibstandarte* had reached St Etienne, where a large enemy garrison surrendered. On the *Leibstandarte*'s flank the soldiers of the *Totenkopf* Division helped mop up the remnants of the enemy, whilst its reconnaissance squadron fought a furious battle with French colonial troops at Tarare, taking some 6,000 prisoners in the process.

RIGHT: Men of the *Polizei* Division rest in a field while awaiting further deployment. The division's first taste of combat came late, when it was employed in assault crossings of the River Aisne at the Ardennes Canal. Once its objectives were secured in this area the division moved on to the Argonne Forest where it fought to capture the town of Les Islettes. This photograph was taken on 18 June 1940. On that day German forces captured Rennes, whilst the 5th *Panzer* Division reached Brest. Two days later, on 20 June 1940, the *Polizei* Division was pulled out and put back in reserve. It remained in France until it was recalled to active duty, being transferred to East Prussia in 1941 to take part in the invasion of the USSR.

LEFT: Soldiers of the *Polizei* Division cross the Ardennes Canal. Bicycles were surprisingly useful – although the troops were seriously impeded over difficult terrain, out in France the countryside was relatively flat and ideal for such methods of transportation. The soldiers are armed with the Kar 98K rifle that has been slung over their backs. This 7.92mm (0.31in) bolt-action Mauser design, dating back to the beginning of the century, was the standard German rifle for most of the war. The rifle had a magazine capacity of 5 rounds, weighed only 4kg (8.8lb) and had a muzzle velocity of 785m/s (2,574ft/s). Despite massive production of the rifles German factories could never keep pace with the demand from the front, so the *SS* also used a variety of captured foreign rifles.

ABOVE: Moving through the Ardennes, a supply wagon crosses a ditch that has already seen some heavy traffic. In order to prevent vehicles from sinking in boggy terrain or to cover up bad road surfaces it was standard practice to lay logs down to allow them to pass over relatively easily. These men are from the *Polizei* Division. Because the division was not motorised and relied mainly on horse-drawn transport, the troops found that advancing through the forests of the Ardennes was challenging. A year later in Russia, the division would be issued a number of tracked vehicles to overcome the problem of moving men, equipment and horses across difficult terrain. Freak downpours, even in France, would hinder horse-drawn transport that the division relied on for supplies. But nothing could prepare the troops for the horrors they would experience on the Eastern Front during the autumn and winter of 1941.

ABOVE: A group of officers attached to the *Polizei* Division meet with one of the division's *SS* photographers in June 1940. Although photographers were an important conduit for transmitting news to the German public via the Propaganda Ministry in Berlin, many of them were given strict orders not to reveal their men undergoing mundane duties, but only to show the mighty *SS* in action, in order portray them in the most heroic light. Consequently, even during life and death situations on the battlefield, photographers were compelled to show posed shots of their men supposedly in action, all the time ensuring that any photograph was a well-composed, correctly focused, good-quality image.

LEFT: An *SS* artillery battalion attached to the *Leibstandarte* seen during the later stages of the Battle of France in June 1940. Although by this stage of the war the *Leibstandarte* was fighting a battle of pursuit, in certain sectors of the front occasional heavy fighting occurred. On 19 June 1940, for instance, the *Leibstandarte*, attached to the 19th *Panzer* Division, had to attack a French barricade on the bridge over the River Allier. Following heavy exchanges of fire, French troops blew it up before the *SS* could secure it. By 22 June the *Leibstandarte* was in action again fighting for the town of St Etienne. Here it once more showed its worth in combat.

RIGHT: A new commanding officer belonging to an unidentified *Leibstandarte* regiment greets his troops in June 1940. The officer is wearing an M1937 field-grey peaked service cap. The badges worn on all *SS* peaked caps consisted of the national eagle and swastika, and the death's-head of the *SS*. The national eagle worn by *SS* officers was of a different design from Army and Navy patterns. The men are wearing the Army-pattern M1940 tunic. The collar patches display the typical wartime machine-embroidered runes on the right, and a black wool patch with the braid rank strip for *SS-Sturmmann* on the left. The shoulder straps are piped in white, but do not display the 'LAH' unit cyphers on the slip-on wool loops.

LEFT: A typical *Leibstandarte* soldier, holding the rank of *SS-Sturmmann*, on guard duty. He is armed with a Kar 98K bolt-action rifle and is wearing the usual rifleman's belt and pouches. His steel helmet is the M1935/40 model with the first pattern runes applied to the right side of the helmet. The runic decal remained a popular feature until it was officially abolished in 1943, but it was still seen at the end of the war. The guard is wearing the enlisted man's M1940 service tunic worn by all soldiers of the *Leibstandarte SS Adolf Hitler*. During the war one of the most prominent pieces of insignia worn by troops belonging to the unit was the 'Adolf Hitler' cuff title. It was worn on the left sleeve and showed the signature of the *Führer* in *Sütterlin* script. It remained basically unchanged from the 1930s right through until the end of the war.

LEFT: Essentially the drive south through France was a mopping-up operation and between 17 and 19 June the *Totenkopf* Division captured some 6,088 prisoners. On 20 June it was noted in the *Totenkopf* war diary that a reconnaissance battalion took the surrender of 1,300 French troops. Despite the fact that the division was held in reserve until June 1940, the French campaign proved that the soldiers of the *Totenkopf* were undoubtedly a credible military formation. But proving their fighting spirit had come with a heavy price. They had suffered very heavy casualties, with the loss of some 1,152 men. Most of the men had risked their lives to achieve what they considered were vital objectives. These were a fanatical group of soldiers who did not believe in the word 'defeat'. Nor did they understand morality and servility on the battlefield against their foe. Consequently the division's propensity for brutality and barbarism could do nothing but detract from their battlefield achievements.

RIGHT: Soldiers belonging to the premier *SS* formation, the *Leibstandarte SS Adolf Hitler*. Originally Hitler's bodyguard unit, the *Leibstandarte* had grown from company size in 1933 to become a reinforced regiment in 1940. It was to end the war as an immensely powerful outsize armoured division. This photograph was taken on 5 June 1940 when a total of 140 German divisions launched the Battle of France. The *Leibstandarte* and *SS-Verfügungs* Divisions formed part of *Panzergruppe Kleist* in the advance on Paris. Throughout the advance the *SS* units were given little respite as they drove southwards in pursuit of the retreating French forces, crossing the Marne on 12 June.

LEFT: Troops rest in a French town during the *Polizei* Division's advance. The *Polizei* Division was primarily a horse-drawn formation, but due to its limited operations in the west this did not seriously curtail its advance. Most of these soldiers have been marching over great distances alongside the plodding horses. The men were absolutely dependent upon these animals and due to the serious lack of vehicles in the German armed services, horses were the only available motive power. But as with all wars it was not only the humans that suffered on the battlefield. Animals too, particularly the horses, were exploited to the full. In most cases on the Western Front these animals were killed either by shellfire or else fell victim to aerial machine-gunning. Many died of exertion from towing guns or supplies. However, it would not be until the war on the Eastern Front that the losses would become enormous, with an average of 1,000 horses a day dying across the vast expanses of the Soviet Union.

RIGHT: Troops relax following heavy fighting inside a French town. These *Polizei* Division men are waiting for orders before resuming their advance. The majority of the troops are still holding their Kar 98K bolt-action rifles, indicating that the area is not yet safe. Shortage of rifles meant that the division used a number of foreign and obsolete types. Among submachine guns, or machine pistols, as the *SS* knew them, the MP38/40 was not extensively used by this particular division until it served on the Eastern Front. However, it did receive small batches of earlier models like the Bergmann MP28. This was a very well crafted weapon and was often regarded by the men who used it as a superior design.

LEFT: Marching along a dusty road, soldiers of the *Totenkopf* Division move southwards to participate in the final defeat of the French Army. This photograph was taken on 14 June 1940, and it was on this date that these men moved south of the Marne. The division had already taken a severe mauling – in the last week of May it had suffered no less than 1,140 casualties, including 300 officers. Losses were so serious that Himmler forced Eicke to accept 300 half-trained officer cadets to enable the division to survive on the battlefield. Once again, the soldiers fought well as they pushed southwards and performed feats of remarkable skill and tenacity. But soon this heroism turned to terrible acts of barbarism. Near Dijon, the *Totenkopf* 5th Company of the 2nd Battalion of the 2nd Regiment became embroiled in a fierce battle against Moroccan troops. Because these soldiers were regarded as racial inferiors and sub-human, all Moroccan troops who surrendered were summarily executed. Throughout this combat zone the *Totenkopf* ruthlessly fought its way southwards, and the only enemy soldiers that managed to surrender to it were white.

BELOW: A group of troops attached to the *Polizei* Division wait whilst their comrades dig a grave for some of their war dead. When there were many burials to be carried out larger mass graves were often dug. The corpses of the soldiers were then individually laid to rest, alongside each other. Earth was then used to cover the bodies before a cross or *SS* rune was placed next to where each of the dead soldiers had been laid. Officers were normally buried in individual graves with full *SS* ceremonial honours. *Polizei* Division losses in France were lower than in other *SS* units primarily due to the fact that the *Polizei* Division was a second rate formation which saw only a limited period of combat against the enemy.

ABOVE: Two soldiers belonging to the *Polizei* Division keeping low in a field in northern France. Although it may seem as if these troops are in action, it is more than likely that this photograph has been posed, as the photographer would otherwise have been in a very exposed position. One soldier is armed with a Kar 98K bolt-action rifle whilst his comrade appears to be armed with an MP38 sub-machine gun. The MP38 weighed 4.1kg (9lb), possessed an effective range of 200m (220yds), and was capable of automatic fire at a rate of up·to 500 rounds per minute. The MP38 proved to be one of the most successful sub-machine guns used during World War II and was used extensively by the *SS*. It not only had a high rate of automatic fire, but soldiers also valued it for being light, portable and extremely durable in combat.

ABOVE: The fall of Paris had brought jubilation to the *SS*. In fact soldiers of the *Leibstandarte* were so overwhelmed when news reached their billets at Etrepilly that in a fever of excitement a number of *SS* men rang the bells of the small village church. Here the fife and drum section from the honour company of the *Leibstandarte* march through Paris on 16 June 1940, soon after the fall of the city. The bandsmen are wearing swallows nests (*Schwalbennester*) or 'musician wings'. These were a traditional item of dress worn by European military musicians. They also served to show, by the use of colour, the wearer's branch of service as well as showing that he was indeed a military musician. The saluting base was located in the Avenue Foch, midway between the Arc de Triomphe and the Port Dauphine.

RIGHT: *Totenkopf* troops in pursuit of the last remnants of the French Army south of the Marne. For ease of carriage the majority of the men have shouldered their rifles. On 14 June 1940 news reached these *Totenkopf* units of the fall of Paris. Although the real battle of France was all but over, these soldiers were still aware of the number of isolated pockets of French resistance in the area. For the next eleven days the *Totenkopf* pushed southwards and became viciously embroiled in several battles. Some of the fighting was so fierce that the *SS* soldiers were compelled to fight house-to-house. Both French and Moroccan troops fought courageously against these elite *Totenkopf* soldiers. In some of the battles French units outnumbered their foe by two or even three to one, but the *Totenkopf's* fanaticism and proven combat success led it constantly to overcome often critical situations and enabled it to neutralise its enemies.

ABOVE: Troops of the *Polizei* Division encamped near the town of Les Islettes. This photograph was taken on 21 June 1940. By this time the division had been pulled out of line into reserve. For nearly a year it would remain stationed in France until it was eventually transferred to the Eastern Front. Despite fighting briefly along side its *SS* comrades in France, the division was not considered to be a genuine *SS* formation. In 1942 in Russia, the division would go through a slight transition and would receive not only *SS* uniforms but also a '4th *Polizei* Division' cuff title in *Sütterlin* script. However, many *Polizei* soldiers still wore *Ordnungs-polizei* or Army uniforms. By the end of the war the *Polizei* Division would have grown to become the 4th *SS Panzergrenadier* Division *Polizei*.

RIGHT: This photograph was taken on 16 June 1940 and shows *Totenkopf* troops moving south of the Marne. In just nine days, the *Totenkopf* Division had rounded up the last remnants of the French Army and sent them to the rear into hastily erected PoW camps. By 25 June the division was assigned to occupation duties south of Bordeaux near the Spanish border. It was in this region that the men of the *Totenkopf* would spend a period of time resting and rebuilding. By the time of the armistice on 25 June other German spearheads had penetrated into what would become the French 'free zone' which the armistice left to the new Vichy government. There were German tanks south of Lyon outside Bordeaux, and for a time German motorised vehicles in Vichy. Both *Wehrmacht* and *SS* troops were now imbued with the magnanimity of victory, and as the armistice took effect, these forces slowly withdrew northwards.

ABOVE: Paris fell to the *Wehrmacht* on 14 June 1940. Two days later, Prime Minister Reynaud resigned and was replaced by Marshal Philippe Pétain. The aged hero of Verdun immediately contacted the Germans requesting an armistice. On the same day German troops were marching in triumph as a victory parade moved along the Avenue Foch in Paris. A parade of the fife and drum section lined the road as they followed troops of General Briesen's 30th Infantry Division. The *Wehrmacht* played a prominent role during the victory parade through Paris and the *SS* that attended this military ceremony were undoubtedly in the minority. In fact, during the campaign in the West the official daily reports from OKW (army high command) mentioned the Army, Navy and Air Force, but never the *SS*. Eventually the *SS* did receive public recognition for its contribution on the Western Front in 1940. Even Hitler himself during one of his speeches to the Reichstag summarised the great battle won in France, and he praised all the German forces that took part in the campaign. He stated to his audience that for the first time 'within the framework of these armies, fought the valiant divisions and regiments of the *SS*'. As a result of the war, he added, 'the German Armoured Corps has inscribed for itself a place in the history of the world; the men of the *SS* have a share in this honour'.

ABOVE: *SS* troops line the Avenue Foch as a military band can just be seen passing round next to the Arc de Triomphe. A motorcyclist together with motorcycle combination leads the marching band. The soldier nearest the camera holding the rank of *Sturmmann* is more than likely attached to the *SS-Polizei* Division. He is wearing his M1935 steel helmet, which indicates that he is probably on guard duty. To his right a number of his comrades stand and watch the ceremony. They are all wearing the M1938 *Feldmütze* or side cap, bearing the *SS* death's head insignia. The victory march through Paris mainly consisted of *Wehrmacht* troops, though the *SS* was represented by the *Leibstandarte*. Although the German victory in the West in 1940 could have been won without the use of the *SS* divisions, these elite troops still played a significant part in the triumph. Their measure of success was not quantity, but quality. With the exception of the *Polizei* Division, there were few infantry formations which the *Wehrmacht* possessed in 1940 that could keep pace with the fast and efficient Panzer Divisions. It was mainly the *SS* formations that managed to keep up with the fast-moving tanks, and with their success in such a gruelling campaign Germany's Aryan elite finally received some degree of acceptance from their Army contemporaries.

THE BALKAN CAMPAIGN

In October 1940 Italy invaded Greece. Within a few weeks, the Italians were driven back into Albania by the Greeks.

Hitler became increasingly unhappy about the state of the Axis position in the Balkans and consequently directed his army commanders to prepare a plan for a German attack on Greece. By mid-December 1940, 'Operation Marita', the codename for the invasion of Greece, was already in its final stages of planning. During the following three months German divisions were moved to southern Romania. In February 1941, the *Leibstandarte SS Adolf Hitler* joined them as part of General List's 12th Army. One month later the *SS Division Reich* (formerly the *SS-VT* Division) was moved from France to Temesvar in southwestern Romania in order to take part in the invasion of Yugoslavia alongside the 2nd Army. The journey to Romania had been a major effort for the troops of the *Reich* Division, with huge

LEFT: *Das Reich* Division soldiers struggle through the mire with a motorcycle combination during the opening phases of the Balkans campaign in April 1941. For this elite *Waffen-SS* formation the advance to Belgrade did not go very smoothly.

traffic jams, units running out of fuel, vehicles breaking down, and overloaded trucks struggling to keep pace with columns over the steep mountains. But despite this inauspicious beginning, these tough fighting men were soon to prove their worth in combat.

On 6 April, following a heavy systematic bombardment of Belgrade, German armoured infantry columns finally poured across into Yugoslavia in their familiar *Blitzkrieg* style. The *Reich* Division was ordered by General Paul Hausser to capture Belgrade at all costs. He sent out an order to his men on 11 April and told them that, '*Reich* must, whatever the circumstances, capture the Belgrade bridges and be the first German troops into the city….' What followed was an arduous drive for a handful of men across the rain-sodden marsh, battling through strong resistance towards Belgrade. Determinedly they forged ahead towards the Yugoslav capital, whilst up above the *Luftwaffe* continuously battered the poorly equipped Yugoslavian Army.

By 13 April, troops of *Reich*'s reconnaissance battalion reached the heavily bombed capital. *Hauptsturmführer* Fritz Klingenberg, a company commander in the battalion, captured the city with just ten men. For his bold and daring action, Hitler awarded him the Knight's Cross. By an equally determined effort, troops belonging to the *Deutschland* Regiment had successfully brought all its battalions through Alibunar and beyond, aware that the Yugoslav defences were rapidly crumbling in front of it.

Meanwhile, in the southern theatre of operations the 12th Army, together with the *Leibstandarte SS Adolf Hitler* and the Army's elite *Grossdeutschland* Regiment, attacked from Bulgaria through Yugoslavia, and then on into Greece. *Leibstandarte* troops ploughed through the meagre Yugoslav defences, out-manoeuvring and out-fighting their opponents until they captured the stronghold of Monastir near the Yugoslav–Greek border. At the Klidi Pass the *SS* were confronted by firmly entrenched British and Australian troops, determined to hold the mountain crests that dominated the pass at all costs. But

yet again the *SS* soldiers proved their courage and zeal and fought a number of fierce battles, some of which were hand-to-hand, until eventually they drove the brave defenders from their positions. By the early afternoon on 13 April 1941, the Klidi Pass was in German hands.

The following day the *Leibstandarte* pushed through in the direction of the Klisura Pass.

Hitler, in a rage, ordered the *Wehrmacht* to 'crush the Slav state with merciless brutality', in a lightning campaign.

Around the Kastoria Pass and Lake Kastoria an *SS* battalion struck a Greek division protecting the British left flank. What followed on the mountain slopes was a series of vicious fights with determined Greek soldiers holding their strong defences to the death. Under the command of Kurt Meyer the men of the *Leibstandarte* were undeterred by the resistance and fought on stubbornly until they overcame the defences. Meyer's battalion took the key town of Kastoria and with it 11,000 prisoners. For his unit's achievements, Meyer was awarded the Knight's Cross.

In the days that followed the battle of Kastoria, the men of the *Leibstandarte* continued to drive retreating columns of confused and disorganised enemy troops. By 20 April 1941, the *SS* had captured the Metzovon Pass, thus sealing the fate of sixteen divisions of the Greek Army. Over the next few days the *Leibstandarte* found itself in hot pursuit of retreating British forces that had moved southwards along the Aegean coast towards Athens. The *SS* units were determined to cut off the remnants of the British force by crossing over the Pindus Mountains to reach the strait of Corinth at Navpaktos. But to their surprise the British had eluded them and evacuated. Meyer, the Reconnaissance Battalion commander, quickly ordered his men into fishing boats at Navpaktos

LEFT: A group of *Waffen-SS* motorcyclists pose for the camera next to a motorcycle combination. Taken on 6 April 1941, the photo shows men of a *Leibstandarte SS Adolf Hitler* motorcycle unit. The *Leibstandarte* was given the task of spearheading the German attack from Bulgaria through southern Yugoslavia and then into Greece. This unit was working closely with the 9th *Panzer* Division and was probably in a reconnaissance role, advancing through Yugoslavia towards Skopje. The soldiers are all wearing the waterproof motorcycle coat. Two have the tail of the coat gathered in around their legs and buttoned into positioned to allow easier and safer movement whilst on the motorcycle. Most of the motorcyclists are wearing the usual rifleman's belt and Kar 98K pouches.

and ferried the advance guard across to the Peleponnese. The remainder of the *Leibstandarte* had meanwhile moved down the west coast road to Pirgos, where a battle group captured an entire British tank regiment. Meyer's Reconnaissance Battalion undertook a series of clearing operations along the Gulf of Corinth and linked up with the 2nd *Fallschirmjäger* Regiment.

On 27 April, German troops finally entered Athens, and before the end of the month the Germans were in full control of the country. The Balkan Campaign for the *SS* was now at an end.

Prior to *SS* troops being moved back to barracks in Czechoslovakia to refit and prepare for their next campaign, units of the *Leibstandarte* were ordered to take part in another victory parade, this time in Athens.

In terms of time and the superior fighting techniques employed by the *Waffen-SS* the campaign in the Balkans had been a great triumph. This elite group of soldiers had yet again fought with great skill, élan and daring. In the face of fierce resistance from tough adversaries the soldiers had battled their way through to victory.

RIGHT: *Waffen-SS* graves in Greece, seen after the successful invasion of the Balkans in April 1941. The lack of good rail and road links, natural obstacles such as hills and mountain slopes, together with bad weather, considerably hindered the *SS* advance. The terrain, as every German tactician was fully aware, was an important factor in operations, with crucial importance to the success of the Army's whole strategy of the war. Planning of the Balkans campaign had been very strongly influenced by the natural obstacles which the German advance would face. Yugoslavia was a land whose sprawling territory contained every type of terrain. It was in the mountain ranges of the Balkans that many *SS* men lost their lives, and would continue to lose their lives, to fanatical resistance.

LEFT: Soldiers of the *SS Division Reich* seen prior to their long journey from France to Temsvar in southwestern Romania. The troops are servicing a 3.7cm (1.45in) Pak 35/36 anti-tank gun in order for it to be ready for action in the Balkans. The Pak 35/36 was the first anti-tank gun to be used by the *Waffen-SS*. Although it had proven its worth in Poland, on the Western Front in 1940 Pak crews soon realized its tactical limitations against heavy enemy armour. Even ten months later in the Balkans, the demand for a more powerful antitank gun was not given priority, and it was not until *Waffen-SS* Pak crews arrived on the Eastern Front that they confirmed the growing need of up-gunning the Pak 35/36. British Matildas and French Char Bs had been bad enough: trying to take on the superb Soviet T-34 and the massive KV-1 with such a weapon which could not penetrate their armour proved to be little short of suicide.

RIGHT: Two children stand next to a Mercedes Medium truck. The licence plate of the vehicle is *SS-70712*. As with all licence plates on German military vehicles the letter prefix groups indicated the organization to which the vehicle was assigned – WH was used by the Army, WK by the *Kriegsmarine* and WL by the *Luftwaffe*. The *Sig* runes on this Mercedes denoted that it belonged to the *Waffen-SS*. This particular *SS* vehicle had been temporarily pressed into service as a school bus prior to it leaving its home station for the Balkans. With the severe shortages of vehicles in the German armed services many civilian trucks were impressed into *Wehrmacht* and *Waffen-SS* divisions as a desperate measure to replace worn-out vehicles and bring army units to their full allotment.

ABOVE: An *SS* flak gunner of the *Leibstandarte* demonstrates the 2cm (0.78in) Flak 38 light anti-aircraft gun in the barracks at Vesoul in eastern France in March 1941. The anti-aircraft gun's main purpose was to deliver a deadly barrage of explosive shells against enemy aircraft, but they were also fearsome anti-personnel weapons. The first *SS* anti-aircraft machine-gun battalion was formed in 1939 for the invasion of Poland. In 1940 the newly activated *SS-Verfügungs* Division received a three-company light anti-aircraft battalion equipped with some 36 2cm self-propelled anti-aircraft guns mounted on halftrack artillery tractors. This particular 2cm anti-aircraft gun is mounted on a converted trailer that was specially designed to be towed by either halftrack or wheeled vehicles. By the time the Balkan campaign began in early April 1941 the number of *SS* anti-aircraft battalions had been increased and by the end of the following month there were no less than 16 independent flak battalions preparing for operations against Russia.

ABOVE: *Waffen-SS* troops pay tribute to their war dead. Although *SS* combat performance exceeded all expectations during the early years of the war, thanks to their intensive pre-war training, casualties on the front lines were surprisingly high. *SS* units generally took too many risks on the battlefield, and large numbers of SS men paid for their daring with their lives. *Reichsführer-SS* Heinrich Himmler summed up their worth: 'Their lives are of value to them only as long as they can be used to serve the *Führer*. They toss them away for all the world as if they were hand grenades when the need, or even the opportunity arises'.

RIGHT: The draped coffin of a fallen *SS* commander is guarded by members of his unit. The *SS* motto *Mein Ehre Heisst Treue* (My Honour is Loyalty) was the foundation of all *Waffen-SS* actions. Every *SS* man swore an oath to carry out any order issued by the *Führer* or by a superior, regardless of the sacrifice involved. As a result, *Waffen-SS* troops had to learn that nothing was considered impossible. Himmler quite clearly stated: '...It is unthinkable that we should one day say to the *Führer*, "We have no more to offer, my *Führer*."' Such unquestioning obedience gave the *Waffen-SS* its distinctive ruthlessness in combat, since its members believed that whatever they did on the battlefield fully justified the means.

LEFT: An *SS* sentry stands guard at the grave of a company commander killed in action. The draped coffin can be seen with an M1935 steel helmet on top. Funerals in the *SS* were tailored to suit Nazi ideology and all *Waffen-SS* soldiers who perished on the battlefield were regarded as war heroes. In the eyes of the *SS* soldier those who died fighting had actually sacrificed themselves in the name of the *Führer*. At Himmler's insistence, every funeral was a kind of Nordic ritual, drawing heavily on the mythology of the Aryan-Nordic race. In fact, many of the rituals used had been invented by the German Romantics of the 19th century and appropriated by the Nazis.

RIGHT: A horch cross country vehicle attached to the *Reich* Division is seen during the Balkans campaign. Note the tactical symbol painted in white on the front left mudguard. Most German military vehicles carried symbols to denote the unit to which they were assigned. These tactical symbols were modified from German military map symbols for various types of weapons and vehicles, and were mainly applied in white. However, other colours were used. Some divisions used white, red, yellow, blue, light green and dark green in order to denote companies, battalions or HQ units within the division. This particular vehicle carries a Red Cross command pennant on the left mudguard.

LEFT: A sniper takes aim through the telescope attached to his Kar 98K sniper rifle. Most German snipers used a x4 or a x6 telescopic sight, the latter being effective at ranges of up to 1,000m (3,280ft). Around 20 snipers were assigned to a battalion, six remaining at the battalion HQ while the others were attached to individual companies. The head of the detachment was responsible for making daily observation reports and recording ammunition usage and kills. Missions were generally ordered at battalion level, but later in the war as the numbers of qualified snipers began to decline more targeting orders were passed down direct from the divisional HQ. Most infantry companies also had some ordinary riflemen whose weapons could be fitted with scope sights.

RIGHT: Transferring from train to road on the way to the Balkans in April 1941. These troops belong to the *Reich* Division and are unloading essential equipment from flat-bed railway cars at Temesvar in Romania ready for the long arduous journey by road. This *SS* unit had already been on the move for a week, having undertaken the long rail journey from southern France to western Romania. For most of the *SS* men, the journey from Temesvar to Belgrade was largely a tiring foot march, with motorcycle and armoured reconnaissance groups probing ahead of the main body to find an accessible route across the Danube so that the corps could advance with the best possible speed.

RIGHT: A group of *Waffen-SS* soldiers prepare to pay their respects to their dead company commander. The mourning wreaths are tied with black ribbons which display the regiment's name. At the end of the ribbon the *SS* runes can be seen. Once the coffin was laid to rest it was not unusual for large *SS* runes to surmount the draped Nazi national flag. Nazis regarded death in battle as heroic, and *Waffen-SS* graves were regarded by the men who honoured them as a place of sanctuary, ennobled by the fallen who had spilled their own blood in the name of the *Führer*. For this reason it was considered that a tomb should never be forgotten. This was a very important part of *Waffen-SS* ritual.

ABOVE: *Leibstandarte* soldiers posing in front of the camera along with *Wehrmacht* troops from the 9th *Panzer* Division during its drive on the Klidi Pass on 11 April. Because of the cold temperatures in the hills all the troops are wearing army standard issue field-grey greatcoats. Under the cover of a heavy systematic barrage against British positions on the Klidi Pass the 9th *Panzer* Division broke through into enemy lines whilst men of the *Leibstandarte* fought hand-to-hand in a savage attempt to drive the British and Imperial troops from their positions. For hours the battle raged as the *SS* attempted to force their enemy from the hills. By 12 April the Klidi Pass was in German hands together with 600 prisoners that had been captured in this vicious battle of attrition. The majority of the prisoners were from the Australian 2nd/4th Battalion and were the first Imperial troops the *Leibstandarte* had come into contact with. The following day soldiers of the *Leibstandarte* drove through the pass and headed in the direction of the Klisura Pass. In marked contrast to their reputation in other theatres, the *SS* units in Greece were considered hard but fair by their enemies.

ABOVE: An officer belonging to the *Leibstandarte* examines a Russian rifle captured from a Yugoslav civilian during the Balkans campaign. The *SS* man is wearing the *Feldgendarmerie* gorget and an officer's *Feldmütze* with the Death's Head badge. By the morning of 9 April 1941 a link-up had finally been made with the Italians by the *Leibstandarte*, now spearheading the corps' advance. The drive through Yugoslavia had been so successful, that since the beginning of the campaign, the *Leibstandarte* had only suffered five casualties, all wounded. But on 10 April, the *Leibstandarte* was ordered to open the Klidi Pass – the gateway to Greece – and strongly dug-in British and Australian troops promised harder times ahead.

LEFT: A posed shot showing a group of *SS Division Reich* men in action with their Kar98K bolt-action rifles. The photo was taken during the opening phases of Operation 'Marita', the codename for the German invasion of the Balkans. Armoured and infantry columns smashed through Yugoslavia from north, south and south-east in the familiar *Blitzkrieg* style. In the north the *Reich* Division drove at speed to take Belgrade. Frantic efforts to mobilise the million-man Yugoslav army were never completed in time. Zagreb fell on 10 April to a combined attack by armoured units and troops of *Reich*. Just three days later Belgrade finally surrendered to an *SS* assault group belonging to *Reich's* Reconnaissance Battalion.

ABOVE: A motorcycle unit belonging to the *Leibstandarte* Division races southwards through Greece following extensive action at Lake Kastoria. The advance of the *Leibstandarte* was then directed along the Servia, but rain and demolitions hindered its drive to such an extent that new orders were issued. On 19 April the division was ordered southwestwards from Gravena to Ioannina in a move to cut off the Greek units holding the line. *Leibstandarte* units then proceeded with all the élan and military skill typical of a top line *SS* formation and captured the Mesovan Pass. In the process the soldiers isolated the Greek units holding positions on the west side of the Pindus Mountains. Within hours the Greek forces crumbled under *SS* pressure which compelled the Greek leaders to sue for an armistice on 21 April. The only organized opposition left in Greece came from British and Empire forces. Soon these were being forced to withdraw as *Leibstandarte* units drove 290km (180 miles), across the Pindus Mountains to the Straits of Corinth – only to find that the British forces had eluded them by evacuation. In spite of this setback the *Leibstandarte* Reconnaissance Battalion commandeered a pair of fishing boats and began a ferry service from Navpaktos, bringing the whole of the *SS* advance guard across the water. The *Leibstandarte* then moved down the west road to Pirgos, where a battle group captured an entire British tank regiment.

LEFT: German officers consider the latest developments in the operation to take the Balkans. Although the Yugoslav Army was weak and poorly equipped and was only ever able to put up a token resistance, German plans were hampered by wet spring weather that reduced the roads to muddy swamps, making rapid movement very difficult. Both the *Wehrmacht* and *Waffen-SS* formations were constantly held up as movement by wheeled vehicles became almost impossible. The race to the Yugoslav capital by the *Reich* Division often slowed to a crawl as the elite formation's vehicles continuously became stuck in the mud. However, bad though the Balkans mud might have seemed, it bore no comparison to the awesome difficulties encountered by German troops six months later in Russia. Not that the troops who remained had it any easier: the Yugoslav Army might have been defeated, but partisans groups sprang up like mushrooms as the Balkans exploded into one of the most vicious guerrilla wars ever fought.

RIGHT: An *SS-Standartenführer* or Colonel inspects a captured Yugoslav trench somewhere in the Balkans in April 1941. He is wearing the *SS Feldmütze fur Führer neuer Art* that was introduced by an order of December 1939, to provide *SS* officers with a soft cap for field wear under conditions where the steel helmet was not required. The field cap could also be easily stowed away if the helmet was put on. *Standartenführers* and higher ranks did not display the *SS* runes on the collar worn by all other ranks. Instead both patches displayed the rank insignia, which consisted of one, two or three embroidered silver oakleaves together with white metal 'pips'.

LEFT: *SS* Division *Reich* troopers stand guard in occupied Belgrade. During the drive on the city there had been considerable competition between *Reich* and the Army's elite *Grossdeutschland* Regiment as to who would arrive at the capital first. Many of the roads leading into the city were blocked. However, this did not prevent a bold action made by *Reich's* reconnaissance commander, *SS-Hauptsturmführer* Klingenberg. With the aid of a captured Yugoslav motorboat he led a small *SS* assault group across the river Danube into the suburbs of Belgrade. Klingenberg seized control of some of the government buildings and by pretending to be the advance guard of a much larger force made the Mayor of Belgrade surrender the city. When the 11th *Panzer* Division entered the capital it was amazed to see it under the military control of no more than a dozen *SS* troops. Following the capitulation of Belgrade the disintegration of the Yugoslav Army rapidly accelerated.

ABOVE: A convoy of *Waffen-SS* halftracks moves along a road in Greece in mid-April 1941. The semi-tracked vehicles are towing 15cm (5.9in) sFH 18 field howitzers. The howitzers are being transported in two pieces. The barrel trailer or 'barrel cart' was positioned low, almost right over the trailer axle, and was drawn back only far enough to maintain the trailer's centre of gravity. The technique of moving the gun in two parts was always considered difficult, and invariably consumed a lot of time. Note the *Feldgendarme* holding a baton in order to give signals to vehicles. This was used like a semaphore flag and it helped to control convoys whilst in radio silence. The *Feldgendarmerie* was a military body that had police powers and formed part of the *Wehrmacht* and *Waffen-SS* in the field. During an advance the *Feldgendarmerie* followed closely behind the fighting troops, erecting military and civil signs, directing traffic, guarding booty, collecting refugees, rounding up enemy stragglers and terrorists. In the *Reich* they were given other duties which included rounding up deserters and military traffic control.

ABOVE: A *Waffen-SS* machine gunner aims twin MG34 machine guns on an anti-aircraft mount. The buffered, specially adapted sustained fire mount gave the pair of guns sufficient stability to reach a maximum range of 2,000m (2,187yds). The circular sight fixed to the weapon enabled the gunner to calculate the lead he must give to an aircraft flying across his line of fire.

The MG34 machine gun was a lethal weapon and it had a tremendous rate of fire of up to 800 to 900rpm (cyclic) per gun. This weapon was more than capable of severely damaging or even bringing down low-level attacking aircraft. It was the first true general-purpose machine gun, equally capable in the sustained fire role and as infantry squad weapon.

LEFT: A *Leibstandarte* mortar crew in action in Greece. They are using a 5cm *leichte Granatwerfer* (leGW) 36 light mortar. It had a calibre of 5cm (2in) and weighed 14kg (30.9lb). It had a muzzle velocity of 75m/s (296ft/s) and fired a small 0.9kg (1.96lb) charge to a maximum range of 520m (596yds). The leGW 36 mortar was used by the *Waffen-SS* until production terminated in 1941 – the weapon was too complex, too expensive and lacked sufficient punch against enemy positions. At the time the photo was taken the *Leibstandarte* had reached Pirgos. It was here that the SS troops captured men of the 3rd Royal Tank Regiment. A unit of the Reconnaissance Battalion then undertook a clearing operation on the southern coast of the Gulf of Corinth and successfully established a link-up with the 2nd *Fallschirmjäger* Regiment which had been involved in bitter fighting with the British at the Corinth Canal.

ABOVE: An sFH 18 heavy field howitzer crew preparing to open fire against British positions in Greece. The heavy weapon has not been dug in and protected against counter-battery fire, which indicates that there is little or no hostile artillery in the immediate area. This piece was capable of firing eight different propellant charges, out to a maximum range of 13,250m (14,500yds). As with most German artillery pieces, the howitzer was very heavy for its size. It was a beast to manoeuvre, but it was nevertheless very effective at dealing with fortified enemy positions. Its high muzzle velocity and weighty shell made it absolutely lethal. Note the mats positioned under the gun's wheels designed to prevent it from sinking into the ground.

RIGHT: A *Reich* reconnaissance unit takes cover behind a verge during operations in the Balkans in April 1941. Two soldiers are using scissor binoculars, calculating the range of their enemy. The scissor binoculars allowed men to observe over the parapet of a trench without the fear of being hit by enemy fire. Because the lenses were further apart than a pair of human eyes, they were able to determine ranges much more precisely.

ABOVE: A group of *Waffen-SS* soldiers pose with captured artillery. The troops are all wearing the standard issue *SS Feldmütze*, and a number of them are equipped with camouflage smocks. The smock was specially designed to be worn over the field equipment. The first pattern smock had side chest vents for access to the ammunition pouches, and the elasticated waist was set low to pull tightly under the belt equipment.

RIGHT: *Waffen-SS* troops man a trench overlooking enemy positions in the Balkans. The men standing left and right are dressed in M37 tunic and trousers, under an early first-type smock in 'palm tree' pattern, summer side out. The actual patterns were, on one side, in summer greens and browns of light, medium and dark shades, reversing to light, medium and dark autumn brown shades. The smocks were very rich in colour. German manufacturers were world leaders in the production of a wide variety of camouflage printed garments, and from 1941 onwards all members of *Waffen-SS* divisions were issued with them. During the war years tunics were standardised, and produced for the *Waffen-SS* in factories run by the *SS-WVHA* economic administration. All *Waffen-SS* uniforms were processed through distribution centres like Buchenwald concentration camp, and inside carried a sinister tag stamped '*SS.BW*'.

The smocks these troops are wearing is the M1940 design with its spring/summer side exposed. These camouflaged garments had a lace-up front opening down to the waist, loosely cut bellows sleeves and two vertical openings at the chest with covering flaps. The waist and wrists were elasticated for a much closer fit. Two large openings each side of the smock were intended to allow the soldier to access his ammunition.

ABOVE: A *Waffen-SS* soldier inside a trench observes enemy positions by using a periscope mirror sight. The *SS* man is unusually wearing the reverse 'autumn' side of the smock, probably trying to blend in with his muddy surroundings. His helmet cover is of 'oak leaf' pattern, with foliage loops. The bayonet for his Kar 98K bolt-action rifle can be seen attached to his belt with cartridge pouches. Although not seen in this photograph, his conventional field equipment would consist of a webbing assault pack hooked to his Y-straps that contained an A-frame to which would be attached his mess tin, gasmask canister with gas cape bag, personal kit, ration bag, and a rolled *Zeltbahn* or rain cape strapped round the outside. Hanging from his belt would be the bread bag, water bottle and entrenching tool. He is more than likely wearing standard marching boots that have been protected with an improvised canvas covering.

LEFT: An officer with the rank of *SS-Standartenführer* (or Colonel) seen after being decorated with the Iron Cross 1st Class for his bravery in the field. He is wearing a number of decorations pinned to his officer's service tunic including Iron Cross 2nd Class, Infantry Assault Badge, silver grade Wound Badge, and the *Deutsches Kreuz* (German Cross), a metal award badge which bridged the gap between the Iron Cross 1st Class and the Knight's Cross. Out in the field many officers preferred the cloth version of the German Cross as it was lighter and less likely to snag on obstacles. The tunic he is wearing is in the pre-war style, with pleated patch breast pockets and slanted lower pockets, and made from a very fine field-green wool material. He is wearing the standard issue senior officer's peaked service cap which displays the *SS* version of the national eagle-and-swastika badge, together with the *SS Totenkopf* or Death's-Head insignia. Both the swastika and *SS* insignia are made from steel finished with a silver wash. Later in the war cheaper versions would be manufactured from aluminium.

RIGHT: Three officers pose for the camera following the decoration of their comrade in the middle with the Iron Cross 1st Class. The *SS-Untersturm-führer* on the right has the Iron Cross 2nd Class pinned to his left breast pocket. He also holds a number of other decorations including an assault badge and the German Cross. He is wearing the standard issue officer's peaked service cap. The newly-decorated *SS-Sturmbannführer* displays the Iron Cross 2nd Class badge, an assault badge and the German Cross award badge. His officer's peaked service cap is of the old model type that was introduced in 1938.The *SS-Obersturmführer* to his right wears the Iron Cross 2nd Class and the German Cross award badge. He is wearing the *SS*-style *Feldmütze*.

LEFT: Two *Waffen-SS* soldiers are dragging a weary horse through water following a heavy Balkan downpour. Movements in April 1941 were severely hampered by the influence of mud. It affected cross-country movement, particularly in areas where some of the stiffest enemy resistance was encountered. The closer *Waffen-SS* troops got to the battle zone, the worse the mud became, for the action of vehicles, especially tracked ones, churned up the terrain into a swamp. Where the going was not boggy it was loose sand, and drivers of horse-drawn transport in particular had to avoid the tracks of lorries, for to follow in these would certainly lead them to become bogged down. The experiences endured in the Balkans were comparable to those that the troops would suffer on the Eastern Front. However, unlike Russia the Balkans proved a rapid conquest and the frustrating mud could be overcome for the enemy were weak and unprepared for war.

ABOVE: An *SS-Gruppenführer* and bearer of the highly coveted Knight's Cross confers with a newly decorated comrade. Both men are highly decorated and have received the Iron Cross 1st Class and a number of other awards. One commander that became very famous in the Balkans was *SS-Hauptsturmführer* Fritz Klingenberg, who was responsible for capturing Belgrade. Awarded the Knight's Cross of the Iron Cross, he quickly became a celebrity in the Third Reich, and soon enthralled listeners on the radio with the dramatic events that led him and his small *Waffen-* SS assault group to the capture of the Yugoslavian capital. Through the rest of the war Klingenberg's star continued to rise, and after distinguishing himself on the Eastern Front, he eventually became the commander of the 17th *Panzergrenadier* Division *Götz von Berlichingen*. However, his high rank and the many awards which had been bestowed upon him for bravery, which made him one of the most famous *Waffen-SS* commanders of the war, did not make him invulnerable, and he was killed in action near Herxheim in the Palatinate in 1945.

RIGHT: A *Waffen-SS* photographer belonging to the *Propagandakompanie* poses for the camera. This photograph was taken near Belgrade on 10 April 1941 and suggests this man may have been one of the official photographers assigned to the *SS Division Reich* during its advance from the Romanian border into Yugoslavia and then on to Belgrade. The *Reich* Division was part of XLI Panzer Corps, under the command of General Georg-Hans Reinhardt, and it was this elite *SS* division that was involved in the thrust on Belgrade. However, the advance was severely hindered by boggy terrain, but divisional commander *SS-Gruppenführer* Paul 'Papa' Hausser believed his troops would be able to reach the Yugoslav capital ahead of the Army's troops. It was for this reason that Hausser insisted that a photographer should follow the *Reich*'s advance through Yugoslavia to record what he regarded as 'an historic moment in his division's crusade'. Hausser's faith was justified, and by 11 April the first soldiers belonging to the *Reich* Division had forced their way across the Danube.

ABOVE: *Leibstandarte* troops wade along a river in Greece. This photograph was taken during the later stages of the campaign in Greece, by which time the *Leibstandarte* had smashed through Greek and commonwealth forces. On 27 April, German troops entered Athens and just three days later they were in complete control of the country. In total some 223,000 Greek and 21,900 British prisoners had been taken. German losses for the entire Balkan campaign amounted to some 2,559 dead, 5,820 wounded and 3,169 missing. Once again, as they had done so in Paris nearly a year earlier, the *Leibstandarte* were ordered to participate in the victory parade, this time in Athens.

ABOVE: Two commanders in a dug-out overlooking the deployment of their forces as they go into action. The man on the left is an *SS-Brigadeführer* (though he is wearing the uniform of a police general) and his comrade is an *SS-Untersturmführer*. Although the campaign in the Balkans had been a grand display of military might using *Blitzkrieg* as the main method of attaining yet another rapid victory, the German invasion of Russia had been postponed, thereby denying German forces almost half of the best campaigning season on the Eastern Front. Nevertheless, morale among *Wehrmacht* and *Waffen-SS* units was high, and the war against the Soviet Union seemed destined for another swift victory. Himmler's *Waffen-SS* had proved that, despite the muddy conditions and unfavourable terrain, the war in southern Europe had almost been a walk-over. Nothing, it seemed, could prevent these elite soldiers from going from one victory to another. They now relished the thought of doing battle against the Red Army.

LEFT: A Pz.Kpfw.III undergoes a field overhaul following the defeat of the Yugoslav Army in April 1941. Up until the Balkans campaign, the *Waffen-SS* relied upon the Army to provide armoured support, but by the invasion of Russia in June 1941 the *Leibstandarte* had acquired a tank *Abteilung* to go along with its new status as a division. The Panzer III was intended to be the standard German battle tank, but though it was an effective design it was no match for the Russian tanks it was to encounter in the months which followed. However, it was capable of being upgunned, and it continued as a frontline weapon until the Battle of Kursk in the summer of 1943.

THE ITALIAN CAMPAIGN

By August 1943, the German Armies in North Africa and Sicily had been defeated and those units that had escaped were now defending the Italian mainland.

A month later, in September 1943, the Allies landed at Salerno, and Anglo-American forces drove slowly northwards against a retreating German Army. However, the German forces carried out a series of successful fighting withdrawals that inflicted massive casualties on the enemy. Those forces included the *Leibstandarte SS Adolf Hitler*, by now a full armoured division, which had been transferred from the battlefield at Kursk in July 1943, leaving its armour and equipment behind in Russia. One of the first tasks on arrival in Italy was to help disarm Italian Army units after the overthrow of Mussolini's government in September 1943. In addition to this the

LEFT: *Waffen-SS* troops rest following their redeployment from the Eastern Front in 1943. Hitler had ordered the transfer of the *SS*-Panzer Corps to Italy following the Italian capitulation in July 1943. This type of sudden shift became characteristic of the employment of the elite *SS* divisions during the remainder of the war, as the *Führer* used them as a 'fire brigade' to reinforce trouble spots.

division saw extensive anti-partisan operations before returning to the Eastern Front in the autumn.

The campaign in Italy had become a grinding war of attrition which the Allies hoped to cut short by making an amphibious assault south of Rome at Anzio. A new *Waffen-SS* division, the 16th *Panzergrenadier* Division *Reichsführer-SS*, deployed several *Kampfgruppe* to reinforce the 14th Army at the beachhead. The commander of the new division was *SS-Brigadeführer* Max Simon, a former regimental commander in Theodor Eicke's *Totenkopf* Division. When the Allies landed at Anzio the new *SS* division was still being put together and so parts of it had to be quickly rushed to the front.

To help contain the advancing Anglo-Americans there were a number of Italian volunteers who served with the *Waffen-SS* formations. One such formation which fought alongside the *Reichsführer-SS* Division at the Anzio/Nettuno bridgehead was an Italian *SS* legion. It eventually became known as the 29th *Waffen-Grenadier Division der SS* and would see action mainly against communist partisans in the region of the Po Valley. Italian volunteers also made up parts of the 24th *SS Gebirgs* Division *Karstjäger*. These were elite mountain troops that spent most of the war fighting against partisans along the Adriatic coast, in the Alps and in the Dolomites.

Italy's mountainous spine offered endless opportunities for defence. All through the Italian campaign the Germans enhanced this natural advantage by incorporating massive concrete emplacements and tank turrets into their defensive lines, which stretched across the Italian peninsula. These defensive lines were almost impregnable, and in spite of their superior numbers attacking Allied armies became embroiled in bloody fighting that sometimes lasted weeks and even months at a time. Allied air superiority posed less of a threat here than in other theatres. Well established on and behind steep, rocky hillsides, neither the *Wehrmacht* nor their *SS* counterparts had little real need to manoeuvre. The Allies undoubtedly enjoyed material superiority during the Italian campaign, but they were fighting a very skilful enemy who had nothing to lose and much to gain by standing firm and battling almost to the last bullet before retreating to a new defensive line and starting all over again.

Fighting in Italy proved to be very costly for both sides. In spite of Italy's sunny reputation, it can get cold and wet in the mountains. The winter weather was a constant hindrance to both sides and forced them into spells of inactivity. The weather also hampered the attacker more than the defender, giving the initiative to the Germans in their well dug-in positions. All throughout 1944, the Germans continued fighting effective delaying actions as they slowly withdrew northward.

In ten days troops of the the 16th *SS-Panzergrenadier* Division killed more than 360 Italians, claiming that they were partisans.

Apart from the original response to the Allied landings, members of the *Waffen-SS* played little part in the conventional war in Italy. They were involved in the guerrilla campaign, however, and their actions left a brutal mark on the Italian population. Stories of the *SS* committing atrocities against civilians abounded. Predictably most of the German reprisals were aimed at those suspected of collaborating with partisans or undertaking guerrilla actions against German units. As a deterrent, *Waffen-SS* soldiers occasionally destroyed entire towns or villages. In fact, the Italian population had become so terrified of the German reprisals that when the Allies marched into Rome on 4 June 1944, crowds stayed away, fearing a last stand by the departing Germans.

Despite the loss of Rome, the bloody fighting in Italy continued. Even though the Germans were in retreat, they continued to set up defensive lines. The Allies had to fight through the Viterbo Line and the Trasimene Line, before reaching the main German defence of northern Italy, the Gothic Line, in early August 1944.

ABOVE: A *Waffen-SS* flak crew open fire with their 8.8cm (3.45in) flak gun against Allied positions following the British and American seaborne invasion south of Rome at Anzio. Note the 'kill' ring markings along the barrel of the gun. These usually took one of two forms: rings painted round the barrel of the gun, or silhouettes or symbols depicting the targets destroyed. Some units, especially those belonging to the *Waffen-SS*, indicated targets or areas of operations like tanks, aircraft, Eastern and Western Fronts. On larger weapons like the 8.8cm flak gun, crews added small labels with the date and type of target destroyed. Some guns were used for years, scoring many hits. On the most widely used guns there were so many barrel rings that it was difficult to count them accurately or find room to paint more.

In spite of the loss of territory, the Italian campaign was actually strategically advantageous to the German war effort, for it tied down large Allied forces who were stalled against fierce and determined troops along the Gothic Line. By Christmas 1944, the Germans were still holding the Line. Allied losses, coupled with terrain and winter weather, meant that once again the Italian campaign came to a halt.

No campaign in the West cost the Allied infantry more than Italy. Most German soldiers were aware that they were holding the enemy at arm's length from the southern borders of the Reich itself, which added further incentive to their defensive efforts. Even so, Allied weight began to tell. Slowly and systemically the Germans were forced from their positions, or were killed where they stood. By the beginning of 1945, the rapid deterioration in the German military and political situation meant that the forces occupying northern Italy were being stretched by the increasing activities of the partisan bands. But despite the success of the new wave of guerrillas, who managed to take control of large parts of northern Italy, both *Wehrmacht* and *Waffen-SS* units continued to stand and fight for every river line as they retreated towards the Austrian border.

By late April 1945, as the Third Reich neared collapse, German commanders knew that an escape through the Alps was almost impossible. Soon, thousands of dishevelled German troops surrendered, weary and broken. *SS-Obergruppenführer* Karl Wolff negotiated a local ceasefire with the Allies. However, some *SS* units continued to fight, ignoring pleas by Army and *SS* commanders to lay down their arms. Even after Germany's unconditional surrender, on 7 May 1945, there were still isolated groups of *SS* soldiers in the mountains of northern Italy determined to fight and die for *Volk, Führer und Vaterland*.

ABOVE: Preparing for its long haul back to the West, armour destined for the Italian Front has been loaded on-board flat cars in mid 1943. These StuG III Ausf.Gs are a small contingent of assault guns scraped together in Russia to support the *Waffen-SS* divisions in Italy. Assault guns like these were among the first heavy armoured vehicles operated by *Waffen-SS* divisions, several batteries being raised in 1941. The StuG III Ausf.G mounted a 7.5cm (2.95in) StuK 40 L/48 cannon. It was used extensively during the later stages of the war serving in some numbers with the main *Waffen-SS* fighting divisions. By the spring of 1943 each of these divisions was equipped with an assault gun battalion of 21 StuG III Ausf.G vehicles which were used extensively on the Eastern Front. For the *SS* troops the StuG III proved a very valuable support vehicle, and it was was also a potent anti-tank weapon. Since they were much cheaper to build than a tank, they were increasingly used as substitutes for Panzers during the last two years of the war.

LEFT: *Nashorn* (Rhinoceros) *Panzerjäger* move forward in dispersed order in Italy in 1944. The *Nashorn* was a dedicated tank destroyer, mounting a deadly long-barrelled 8.8cm (3.45in) Pak 43 L/71 gun, which was the most effective German anti-tank weapon of its time. On the Eastern Front *Nashorn* crews were able to destroy Soviet T-34 tanks at ranges of up to 4,000m (4,375yds). Operated mainly by independent Army *Panzerjager Abteilungen*, the *Nashorn* was deployed to support specific operations by *Wehrmacht* or *SS* units. When operating in the anti-tank role, the *Panzerjäger* were invariably supported by *Panzergrenadiers*. Later in the war they were replaced by more heavily armoured tank hunters such as the Panzer IV-based *Jagdpanzer*, the even heavier *Jagdpanther* and by small numbers of massive *Jagdtigers*.

ABOVE: The main armoured element of *Waffen-SS* Panzer units was the Pz.Kpfw.IV. This photograph was taken in 1943 and shows Pz.Kpfw.IV tank crews belonging to the *Leibstandarte* then forming part of the II *SS Panzer* Corps in Italy. When the *Leibstandarte* left the Eastern Front it handed over its remaining 39 Pz.Kpfw.IV to the *Das Reich* and *Totenkopf* Divisions, and collected 60 brand new Pz.Kpfw.IV Ausf H tanks in Italy upon its arrival. These tanks are part of the new batch of Pz.Kpfw.IVs that were delivered to the *Leibstandarte* Division. Because of the local terrain the vehicles have been painted with a camouflage scheme of light green spots over the dark sand base. The turret and track side skirting were added to provide protection against anti-tank projectiles, and by the pristine condition of these examples the tanks have yet to see combat. However, during the *Leibstandarte's* three-month stay in Italy the Pz.Kpfw.IV distinguished itself in the dogged fighting around the Allied landings at Anzio.

ABOVE: A *Waffen-SS* flak crew identifies an enemy target during operations in Italy. The gun is a 3.7cm (1.45in) Flak 36 anti-aircraft gun and has been draped with foliage in order to conceal it from aerial observation. The 3.7cm Flak 36 weighed 1,757kg (3,858lb). It was mounted on a cruciform platform giving 360-degree traverse, and fired a 0.56kg (1.2lb) shell to a vertical height of 4,785m (5,235yds) or to 6,492m (7,100yds) against ground targets. Rate of fire was 160 rounds per minute. The *Waffen-SS* began receiving its first medium batteries equipped with 3.7cm guns in July 1941. By the time *Waffen-SS* units had been deployed for operations in Italy in 1943 several new and improved anti-aircraft weapons joined the *SS* flak arsenal, including self-propelled 3.7cm medium anti-aircraft guns and quadruple 2cm (0.78in) guns.

LEFT: Two *Leibstandarte* officers are seen during anti-partisan sweeps in September 1943. The partisan war was fought with great ferocity on both sides, and *SS* units were guilty of a number of atrocities in northern Italy. The security element of the *SS* also left their mark on the Italian population. *SS-Obersturmbann-führer* Herbert Kappler of the *SD-Sicherheitsdienst* (Security Service) had some 330 civilian hostages rounded up in a reprisal raid for the killing by partisans of 32 members of an *SS* police unit in Rome in March 1944. All the civilians were herded into a cave outside the city and executed by pistol shots in the head. The caves were then dynamited and sealed.

ABOVE: Two *Waffen-SS* officers belonging to the *Leibstandarte* confer as they walk along a dusty mountain road in northern Italy in 1943. The *Leibstandarte* was the only one of the 'classic' *SS* divisions to serve in Italy, where it took part in the disarming of Italian Army units following the overthrow of Mussolini's regime in September 1943. The division also undertook major anti-partisan action before returning to the Eastern Front in the autumn of that year. In addition to the German *SS* units there were a number of Italian volunteers who served in *Waffen-SS* formations. These included the Italian *SS* Legion, which saw extensive action fighting alongside units of the *Reichsführer-SS* Division in the region around Anzio and Nettuno. This unit of Italian fascists performed so well that it was even mentioned in the *Wehrmacht* war reports. In 1944 the division was re-named the 29th *Waffen-Grenadier Division der SS*. It spent the largest part of its operational life fighting against communist partisans in the Po Valley area.

ABOVE: A group of *Waffen-SS* troops on a mountain road in Italy in 1944. These soldiers more than likely belong to the 16th *SS-Panzergrenadier* Division, given the honourary title of *Reichsführer-SS*. A motorcycle combination and a Horch light cross-country car can be seen halted on the road. The origins of the division dated back to 1941, when a combat unit was formed from the guard battalion of Himmler's command staff. The *Begliet Bataillon Reichsführer SS* fought in Russia, where it was expanded to form a *Sturmbrigade*. In October 1943 the unit was expanded to form a division, though it was only two thirds the size of a full fighting division. It was still undergoing training when elements were thrown into action at Anzio.

ABOVE: Two *Leibstandarte* riflemen are seen during anti-partisan actions in northern Italy. The partisan war was fought mercilessly by both sides, and the *Leibstandarte* played a leading role in barbaric measures against the Italian population. In September 1943 the town of Boves experienced savage reprisals at the hands of the *Waffen-SS*. The town was almost totally obliterated and its population murdered in cold blood. Although it had been diminished severely by losses during the Battle of Kursk, and it was only in Italy for a short period of time, the crack *SS* troopers were nonetheless welcomed by dwindling *Wehrmacht* formations that were in desperate need of reinforcement against the Allied 5th and 8th Armies.

LEFT: In action – a brigade of *Waffen-SS Nebeltruppe* have just prepared their heavy 21cm (8.3in) *Nebelwerfer* 42 rocket launchers for an attack on Allied positions in northern Italy. Note the troops running from their launchers as their fearsome rockets are about to be launched. It was not until 1941 that German rocket launchers were introduced in any great numbers. Two years later, in 1943, the *Waffen-SS* raised its first rocket launcher battalions armed with the 15cm (5.9in) *Nebelwerfer* 41. The battery, however, is using the heavier and more rare 21cm *Nebelwerfer* 42 seen here, which weighed 1,100kg (2,420lb). The *Nebelwerfer* 42 was a deadly weapon and could fire a full salvo in just eight seconds and three full salvoes in under five minutes.

TOP LEFT: Moving through an orchard a *Waffen-SS* StuG III Ausf.G is seen during operations in northern Italy in 1944. As with all assault guns, the StuG provided the *SS* with vital fire support as the troops went into action. When the three original *Waffen-SS* divisions – *Leibstandarte*, *Das Reich* and *Totenkopf* – were upgraded as *Panzergrenadier* divisions, they received an assault gun battalion of 21 StuG III Ausf.G vehicles. The StuG III provided crucial firepower for *SS* grenadiers. The assault guns were not only robust, but also mechanically reliable and effective, even in hilly terrain like northern Italy. Although the vehicle lacked the all round firepower provided by the rotating turret of a tank, it was less of a drawback during this period of the war, since most armour was deployed in fixed defensive roles. One advantage the assault gun had was that it could carry a longer, heavier and more powerful gun than a tank of similar size.

BOTTOM LEFT: At the beginning of the war the *SS* was very much the poor relation of the army when it came to equipment, but by 1943 the top *SS* divisions were at the front of the line for new weapons like the massive Pz.Kpfw. VI Tiger I. The example seen here is passing a group of *Waffen-SS* troops with captured Soviet M1942 ZIS-3 76mm (3in) artillery on a road somewhere in northern Italy. By this period of the war both the *Wehrmacht* and *Waffen-SS* utilised captured artillery as expansion and production shortfalls compelled them to look for alternative sources of weaponry. In many cases, Soviet artillery was better than its German equivalent. Captured guns usually outranged German pieces, while at the same time being much lighter and more easy to handle for a given calibre.

ABOVE: A *Waffen-SS* crew manning a 7.5cm (2.95in) Pak 40 heavy anti-tank gun. In service this proved to be a deadly and powerful weapon, especially in the hands of well-trained *SS* anti-tank gunners. The gun weighed 1,425kg (3,142lb) in action and had a maximum range of 2,000m (2,188yds). It could penetrate 94mm (3.7in) of armour at 1,000m (1,094yds). As with all anti-tank weapons employed by the *Waffen-SS* these became an integral part of battlefield measures to counter enemy armour. It not only proved an economical and effective counter to the firepower and mobility of enemy armoured formations, but it also provided defensive staying power for *SS* units that were confronted by ever-increasing numbers of ever more powerful enemy tanks. Deficient in anti-tank weaponry during the early years of the war, the *Waffen-SS* were eventually provided with some of the most lethal and novel anti-tank weapons of World War II.

RIGHT: A Pz.Kpfw VI Tiger I tank advancing along a dirt track somewhere in northern Italy in 1943. As with other theatres of war *Waffen-SS* tank crews dominated the battlefield during the latter half of the war with their heavy tanks like the Tiger and Panther. Heavily armoured, the Tiger was armed with the immensely potent 8.8cm (3.45in) KwK 43 L/56 gun. The Tiger entered operational service in August 1942 and by winter 1942–3 the *Waffen-SS* had acquired their first examples. In July 1943 the I. *SS-Panzer* Corps, which had used its Tigers at Kursk, was in the process of creating the *Schwere SS Panzer Abteilung* I. *SS-Panzer,* equipped with 27 Tigers. This *SS* Tiger Company was attached to the *Leibstandarte* as it was sent to Italy. There it was operational until mid-October, when it was transferred back to the Eastern Front.

RIGHT: A wide variety of vehicles on board flatcars bound for the Italian front in 1944. Behind the Pz.Kpfw VI Tiger I is an example of the much acclaimed Pz.Kpfw.V Panther Ausf.G. Although few Panthers served in Italy, which was difficult terrain for prolonged tank operations, both *Wehrmacht* and *Waffen-SS* armoured crews realised that the Panther could be a formidable defensive weapon operating out of dug-in positions. Indeed, it was soon discovered that you did not need the tank, just the turret. Many Panther ground turrets were emplaced. They consisted of the standard Panther turrets and their 7.5cm (2.9in) guns, which were mounted over a rectangular steel box dug into the ground. Italy was never a country that favoured extensive tank operations like the open

steppes in Russia and the plains of France after the breakout of Normandy, but the Panther in particular proved itself in a defensive role.

ABOVE: A Pz.Kpfw.VI Tiger I on board a railway flatcar destined for the Italian Front. In the face of Allied air supremacy, travelling by daylight was hazardous and losses during transportation were high. In under three years of service, the Tiger left an overwhelming impression on its opponents. The *SS* crew's skill and determination helped create 'Tiger-phobia' in Allied units, and some British and American tank crews were reluctant to engage the big German machine. *Waffen-SS* Tiger units constantly made valuable contributions to the German defence of Italy. All the *SS* Tigers in Italy in 1943 were attached to the *Leibstandarte*. Remaining *SS* Tigers were used by the *Das Reich* and *Totenkopf* Divisions in the East.

RIGHT: A Pz.Kpfw.VI Tiger I during operations in Italy in 1943. This 56 tonne (55.1-ton) beast has its external surfaces coated in *Zimmerit* anti-magnetic paste and the whole vehicle is painted in dark yellow. The crew applied camouflaged stripes and patches of dark green, which helped conceal the tank against the Italian terrain. Foliage has also been applied to break up the distinctive outline. Although the mountainous terrain of Italy constantly hindered large-scale offensive tank operations, the terrain favoured the use of tanks in defensive positions. For this reason the Germans took full advantage of the Tiger's power by incorporating Tiger tanks into special defensive emplacements across the Italian peninsula. The use of the Tiger made these positions formidable obstacles to

Allied attackers. German forces used these prepared defensive lines to make the Allied push up the Italian peninsula as costly as possible.

ABOVE: An independent *Waffen-SS* maintenance company overhauls a Tiger I in Italy. The Tiger battalions owed much of their success on the battlefield to well-equipped maintenance companies that kept these complex armoured vehicles in fighting condition. This particular Tiger appears to be undergoing a major overhaul of its turret. Note that the turret is still fitted with smoke dischargers, which were discontinued in mid 1943. The Tiger's biggest fault was its lack of mobility – maximum cross-country speed was just 20kph (12.5mph), and was often considerably less on moderately steep gradients. Although its powerful 8.8cm (3.45in) KwK 36 L/56 gun could easily deal with Allied tanks, turret traverse was notoriously slow.

ABOVE: A *Waffen-SS* Tiger drives through a bomb-damaged town in 1943. This particular tank is painted in overall dark sand with a very light camouflage pattern of green patches. The tactical number is 'S21' and has been painted in yellow on the side of the turret skirting. Note the stowage bin on the rear of the turret. The tank's muzzle brake has a protective cover over it, indicating that fighting is not expected. This cover protected the bore of the barrel from sand, dirt and water. The crew are wearing the red-green *SS-*

Panzer denims with the large patch pockets – Army panzer crews traditionally wore black. This two-piece denim suit was hard wearing, light and easily washable. It was intended to be used during the summer months, especially in warm climates, as a separate item of clothing. The Panzer crews also used it as an outer garment worn over the Panzer uniform. Normal insignia, including shoulder straps and Panzer *Totenkopf* collar patches as well as military decorations, were worn on the jacket.

LEFT: An early model Pz.Kpfw VI.Tiger I moving past a farmstead somewhere in northern Italy in 1943. Four of the five-man crew are taking in the fresh air, only the driver perforce remaining inside. In warm weather tank crews invariably spent lots of time out of the claustrophobic interior of the tank. Unusually, these tankmen are still wearing the old black Panzer uniform with black *Panzer Feldmütze,* based on the standard Army equivalent. By this period of the war virtually all *SS* Panzer crews had opted to wear the *SS* camouflage armoured crew overalls, more suitable for concealment when away from the vehicle.

ABOVE: An Sd.Kfz.251 halftrack pulls alongside a Tiger during operations in Italy. Developed as an armoured personnel carrier for use by Panzergrenadiers, this vehicle was not issued to the *Waffen-SS* until 1942, when the *Leibstandarte*, *Das Reich* and *Totenkopf* were upgraded to *Panzergrenadier* divisions. The half-track carried a complete ten-man *SS* rifle squad plus their machine gun, and it was able to deliver and drop the riflemen at the edge of the battlefield. Tactical employment of the armoured halftrack evolved throughout the war. Initially, *Waffen-SS Panzergrenadiers* moved ahead of the armour and pro-tected the flanks in order to guard against enemy counterattacks as the Panzers smashed their way through the enemy defences. However, by 1943, as the Germans lost the strategic initiative, Panzergrenadier tactics changed. The task of the Panzergrenadiers was now to neutralise enemy tank-destruction parties and anti-tank gun nests. On the Italian Front the halftrack proved its worth and was always on hand to transport *SS* troops to the forward edge of the battlefield, where they were able to debus and attack fixed enemy defences whilst the halftrack provided them with valu-able fire support. By 1944 the *SS-Panzergrenadiers* became more reliant on support by tanks, as halftracks increasingly proved more vulnerable to enemy fire, but the versatile halftrack continued to be used right up until the end of the war.

BELOW: Seen in the Po valley, this camouflaged 2cm (0.78in) *Flakvierling* 38 quad-barrel self-propelled anti-aircraft gun is mounted on the back of a halftrack artillery tractor. The *Flakvierling* could release a hurricane of fire against ground and aerial targets, and was lethal against low-flying aircraft and light armoured vehicles. It could fire 30 explosive 20mm rounds per second from all four of its barrels. Each gun had a muzzle velocity of 900m/s (2,951ft/s) with a maximum ceiling range of 2,200m (7,221yds). The gun proved adaptable, and was used to arm U-boats and warships as well as land units. However, *Luftwaffe*, *Wehrmacht* and *Waffen-SS* crews found the halftrack artillery tractor gun platform very difficult to manoeuvre around. As this photograph shows, the sides of the gun platform could be folded down to provide additional working space for the crew. Magazines for the four guns were carried in ready racks on the folding sides of the platform, and the halftrack usually towed a single-axle trailer, carrying additional ammunition.

RIGHT: An *SS* soldier supports an injured comrade during bitter fighting at Anzio. These troops belong to the newly created 16th *SS Panzergrenadier* Division *Reichsführer-SS*. The Sd.Kfz.251 halftrack with covered MG34 machine gun belongs to an unidentified *Wehrmacht* unit. The *Reichsführer-SS* remained in combat in the Anzio/Nettuno bridgehead until 9 March 1944. Most of the division was then transferred to Hungary to depose the Horthy government. But as the Allies continued to advance through Italy the division returned and was engaged in heavy defensive fighting for the remainder of 1944. *Reichsführer-SS* notoriously played its part in the guerrilla war, unleashing a reign of terror against civilians as it mounted anti-partisan sweeps. Division troops committed a number of large-scale massacres at Padule di Fucecchio and Santa Anna di Stazzema. They also murdered civilians in Marzabotto in September 1944. The Germans later claimed that the civilians had not been executed, but had been hit by crossfire during savage fighting between *SS* troops and partisans.

RIGHT: A 7.5cm (2.95in) Pak 40 heavy anti-tank gun and an MG42 machine gunner take up defensive positions along a road in northern Italy. The MG42 was widely used by the *Waffen-SS*. Based on the MG34, but simplified for ease of manufacture, the MG42 was accurate and had an astonishingly high rate of fire. One of the greatest machine gun designs in history, with superb handling and good reliability, it could be used in all types of terrain and climate. Allied troops soon learned to respect and fear the distinctive snarling sound of the MG42, often described as being 'like Linoleum tearing, but louder'. Formidable in defence when used on a sustained fire tripod, it was also light enough to be used as the principal weapon of the infantry squad when it was fitted with a bipod, as

shown here. One machine gunner reckoned that the rest of the squad's main purpose was 'to carry extra ammunition for my MG42'.

ABOVE: A *Waffen-SS* Pak 40 crew conducts a training exercise on the Gothic Line in the autumn of 1944. The *SS* used this weapon extensively and it became particularly effective against Allied armour. The Pak 40's 7.5cm (2.95in) projectile could easily penetrate the armour of most Allied tanks. Pak batteries were used to break up or stop enemy armoured attacks, whilst *Wehrmacht* and *Waffen-SS* soldiers quickly counterattacked to push back any enemy infantry, which had advanced into the line. Pak crews soon found that the weapon they were using was really too powerful, since it became unstable on firing. However, the *SS* still continued using the gun and it was deadly in the hands of a well-trained crew.

BELOW: A specially converted Sd.Kfz.7/1 halftrack which has had a pair of 2cm (0.78in) Flak 38 anti-aircraft guns mounted. This flak crew have been employed near the Gothic Line and are using their 2cm Flak 38 in a ground role. The Gothic Line stretched from Pesaro on the Adriatic across the Italian peninsula north of Florence to Massa on the Mediterranean. The Germans had cleverly constructed this heavily fortified line in order to delay as long as possible the Allied advance. It was a formidable series of obstacles that included literally hundreds of steel shelters for supporting infantry, along with rock tunnelling with carved defensive embrasures and thousands of mines. The line was also very heavily defended with Panther turrets embedded in rock or set in thick concrete. Houses and farms were gutted and tanks and self-propelled guns were then concealed inside with only their barrels exposed, training on a wide exposed area in front. The Allies reached the Gothic Line in December 1944, but did not mount a final assault until the line was breached in April 1945 at considerable cost in men and material. The defenders had nowhere left to go, and it would only be a matter of weeks before the German Armies in Italy would have to surrender.

THE NORMANDY CAMPAIGN

As the Allied invasion loomed ever closer, the 12th *SS Panzer* Division *Hitlerjugend* was deployed to the Normandy sector.

Just prior to the Allied landings, the division moved into assembly areas around Falaise. Apart from a veteran core of officers and NCOs, these youngsters were largely unblooded, but most were excited at the prospect of fighting. As each day passed during that hot summer of 1944, the tempo of defence preparation increased. A number of exercises were called off, as it was believed the Allied invasion was imminent.

During the early hours of 6 June, following reports of an invasion, *Oberbefehlshaber* (CinC)

LEFT: Young soldiers of the 12th *SS Panzer* Division *Hitlerjugend* move forward in the Normandy sector in June 1944. To get to the invasion beachhead from its base around Lisieux, the division had run the gauntlet of continuous Allied fighter attacks, which disrupted the cohesion of many of the marching columns. One member of 13 *Kompanie* recalled: '*Hitlerjugend*'s advance was punishing. Air attacks wrought death and confusion everywhere.' Regimental commander *SS-Standartenführer* Kurt 'Panzer' Meyer narrowly escaped from his vehicle when it was bombed en route to the front.

West placed both the fifteenth and the seventh Armies on highest alert; at the same time, he ordered the 12th *SS-Panzer* Division *Hitlerjugend* to prepare to march, along with the Army's *Panzer Lehr* and the 17th *SS-Panzergrenadier* Division. Throughout the first morning, convoys of trucks and tanks belonging to the 12th *SS-Panzer* Division *Hitlerjugend* navigated the congested narrow roadways of Normandy, moving northwards bound for the city of Caen and surrounding areas. On its march, vehicles were constantly strafed by fighters, disrupting the cohesion of many of the marching columns. By 7 June, exhausted from more than a day's constant marching, *SS-Standartenführer* Kurt Meyer ordered his soldiers into combat. From their freshly dug trenches, the teenagers crashed into action, opening a ferocious barrage of fire on British and Canadian positions. The fighting was at close quarters, the boys pitching grenades and pumping machine gun fire into the enemy lines.

The *Hitlerjugend* was the first *Waffen-SS* unit to go into action in Normandy. The newly-formed 17th *SS-Panzergrenadier* Division *Götz von Berlichingen* was also ordered to the invasion front, but the *Leibstandarte,* which was still in Belgium, was held back to guard against possible landings in the Pas de Calais. It was eventually released, but did not see action for 11 days, when it was committed to battle around Caen. The 2nd *SS-Panzer* Division *Das Reich* (formerly the *Reich* Division) remained in the south of France in expectation of a possible Allied attack there. However, it was quickly ordered to Normandy.

Das Reich's march north was bathed in blood. This powerful formation was hounded for every mile by the French Resistance. The *SS* men, who had learned their trade in some of the heaviest fighting on the Eastern Front, responded with a series of savage reprisals, which included the massacre of the entire village – including women and children – of Oradour sûr Glane. The division finally reached the Normandy area by 10 July, and was moved into the line near Periers.

It soon became clear to German commanders that the Allies were aiming to take Caen. On the night of 8 June, Panther tanks of *Hitlerjugend*, led by Meyer on a motorcycle, smashed into the Canadian 7th Brigade. Over the next few days the *SS* soldiers fought on fiercely until the *Panzer Lehr* Division moved into line alongside the exhausted boy soldiers. The experienced Army division had been seriously mauled after driving to the front from Chartres. It had lost over 80 self-propelled guns, 130 trucks, five tanks and a multitude of other armoured vehicles to Allied air attack.

Fighting continued to rage around Caen. Through the lanes and farm tracks that criss-crossed the Normandy countryside, rows of dead from both sides lay sprawled out amid a mass of smashed and burned-out vehicles. The fighting here helped create the legend of the fanatical *Hitlerjugend* Division.

'Spitfires attack my company. Cannon and rockets wreak havoc. An infantryman lies on the road and blood streams from his throat. A bullet has severed an artery. He dies in our arms.'

Kurt 'Panzer' Meyer

Over the next few weeks the fighting around Caen intensified. Little mercy was shown or expected from those *SS* soldiers conducting a last-ditch defence. The original invasion plan had called for the capture of Caen within two days: so far the battle had lasted for more than a month. But by 9 July the battle of Caen was all but over, and two days later the 12th *SS* were relieved by the *Leibstandarte Adolf Hitler* Division. Most of the *Hitlerjugend* were pulled back to a rest area between Sassy and Bons. But their rest was to be brief and the boys of the 12th *SS* were soon back in action trying to deny the British a major breakthrough.

The Norman countryside itself actually created conditions favourable to the Germans. The tall hedgerows flanking sunken lanes channelled Allied armoured spearheads. Aided by this terrain the *SS* troops could hold their sector to the grim death. However, savage air attacks and naval bombardment constantly hampered movement and caused unprecedented damage and destruction to armoured vehicles that were desperately needed to sustain the war effort in the West.

On 29 July, units of the *Das Reich* and *Götz von Berlichingen* Divisions successfully smashed through an American armoured regiment near St Denis le Gast, but the attack soon foundered as the troops found themselves overwhelmed by enemy counterattacks. By the beginning of August the *Wehrmacht* together with the *Waffen-SS* were disintegrating. Corps and divisions remained in action on paper, but they were becoming a collection of small battle groups, shrinking down to battalion size.

As the Americans broke out and the Normandy campaign became mobile, catastrophe threatened. To save the German forces in Normandy from being completely encircled and annihilated a series of withdrawals were made through the Falaise–Argentan gap. On 16 August German forces continued their retreat and crossed the River Orne. The *Hitlerjugend* Division desperately battled to keep open the gap. The bulk of the German armour, however, was still trapped in the shrinking Falaise pocket. By 21 August 1944, the battle for the Falaise Pocket was over and the *SS* had been dealt a massive blow.

The Normandy campaign had been a costly one for the *Waffen-SS*, with many of its finest units being all but destroyed. *Das Reich* had some 450 men and 15 tanks left; the 9th *SS-Panzer* Division *Hohenstaufen* had 460 men and some 25 tanks surviving. The 10th *SS-Panzer* Division *Frundsberg* lost all of its tanks and artillery. The *Hitlerjugend* Division only had 300 men remaining with 10 tanks and no artillery.

Following the comprehensive German defeat in Normandy, remnants of its forces were withdrawn for rest and refitting. The *Leibstandarte* was withdrawn to Aachen, *Das Reich* limped back into Germany to the Schnee Eifel area, the *Hitlerjugend* pulled back east of the Maas and *Götz von Berlichingen* was relocated to Metz. The *Hohenstaufen* and *Frundsberg* Divisions were withdrawn

ABOVE: A *Hitlerjugend* grenadier keeps watch in the Caen sector of Normandy. By the morning of 7 June 1944, exhausted from more than a day's forced march under constant air attack, the bulk of the 12th *SS-Panzer* Division had moved into the area north of Caen. This was directly in the path of the British and Canadian armies advancing from the beaches. The city had already suffered considerable damage by heavy allied aerial bombardment, and many of the streets, blocked by huge mounds of rubble, were considered impassable to armour. But the *SS* men were determined not to fight an urbanized battle. Their objective was to hold the city at all costs.

to lick their wounds in a quiet backwater in Holland. It was a town called Arnhem.

In spite of their virtual destruction, the *Waffen-SS* in Normandy had proved yet again that they were amongst the toughest fighting men in the world. But in the face of massive Allied numbers, the *SS* soldier in Normandy could only delay the enemy, not defeat him.

Within months of its defeat in Normandy the *Waffen-SS* would once again see extensive action. However, this time it was not to be a delaying action: this time, the *SS* men were to go on to the offensive in a bold and daring attack through the Ardennes region.

109

ABOVE: 12th *SS-Panzer* Division troops wade through a marsh in northern France. By late afternoon of 7 June 1944 the British forces advancing on Caen had been held back from their target, but the *SS* men had been unable to push them back into the sea. They had been driven back north and northwest of Caen with significant losses in men and material. Instead the 12th *SS* started digging defensive positions, since it was clear that the Allies were not finished in their attempts to

RIGHT: Rudolf Schaff of the 1716th Artillery said that: 'the *SS* showed that they believed that, thus far, everyone had been fighting like milkmaids'. He watched the soldiers of the *Hitlerjugend* Division riding forward into attack, and saw some of them return exhausted that night, 'crying with tears of frustration, not at their losses but for their failure to reach their objective – the sea.' Over the next few days the soldiers of the 12th *SS* Division came under increasingly heavy attacks, the most devastating of which were the heavy shells being fired by battleships offshore. The shelling had become so intense that Panzer shelters were reconstructed into bunkers. During the evening of 9 June, the elite *Wehrmacht Panzer Lehr* Division, commanded by *Afrika Korps* veteran Fritz Bayerlein, moved into line alongside the 12th *SS*. Allied air attacks meant that *Panzer Lehr* had lost over 80 self-propelled guns, 130 trucks, five tanks and a multitude of other armoured vehicles before even reaching the combat zone. For all its misfortunes, *Panzer Lehr* along with the 21st *Panzer*

take Caen. That night, crews of the 5th *Panzer* Company shared the rations they had 'liberated' from wrecked Canadian tanks – food the like of which many had never seen. In addition to the usual canned meat and vegetables, they ate luxuries like peanuts and real chocolate. Afterwards, the boys settled down tired and worn, but far from beaten. Amid all this bloodletting, they had finally become real soldiers. But their achievement had come at a heavy price in lives.

Division and the 12th *SS-Panzer* Division provided the German high command with a tough, experienced armoured core around which to build the defence of the Caen sector – a defence which was to play havoc with Allied invasion timetables.

ABOVE: MG34 gunners in action in Normandy in June 1944. The main gunner – *Schütze 1* – was normally the most experienced and decorated grenadier in the squad. His team mate, *Schütze 2*, fed the ammunition belts and saw that the gun remained fully operational. The machine gun was the infantry squad's chief offensive weapon: the main task of the rest of the squad's riflemen was to carry ammunition for the machine gun. Other members of the squad that normally consisted of two men were generally in charge of bringing up fresh ammunition for the gun. The MG34 was an excellent weapon, built to a very high standard. It had a high rate of fire (but not as high as that of its successor, the MG42). Along the Allied front lines soldiers had the greatest respect for the German machine guns and their highly trained crews. They also learned to respect the fanatical dedication of the teenaged members of the 12th *SS-Panzer* Division. From their hideouts and freshly dug trenches, the boys of the 12th

SS emerged to take the fight to the enemy at the closest of close quarters before withdrawing. They used Eastern Front tricks taught by their veteran cadre, seeming to withdraw only to lead pursuing troops into ambushes. In the nearby village of Malon, the boys took up defensive positions, stalking enemy tanks with their deadly *Panzerfaust*, and destroying several of them. In total the young grenadiers knocked out 28 British and Canadian tanks without loss of their own. Many of the Allied soldiers were shocked at seeing teenagers in *SS* uniforms. It was their first encounter with the *Hitlerjugend* generation. Journalist Chester Wilmot remarked that: 'the troops of the 12th *SS*, who were holding this sector, fought with tenacity and ferocity seldom equalled and never excelled during the whole campaign'. A British tank commander said that they sprang at Allied tanks 'like wolves, until we were compelled under the murderous rain of their fire to kill them against our will'.

ABOVE: An unidentified *Waffen-SS* unit buries its dead in northern France following heavy attacks by the advancing Allies. During the first days of the battle for Normandy German troops tried to prevent the Allies from forming a firm beachhead, but they were not strong enough to force enemy infantry and armour to retreat. By 14 June, losses were mounting to unsustainable proportions. Death and devastation littered almost every road. Within a few days of the invasion it was realized by the Germans that unless reinforcements arrived to help fill these widening gaps in the

disintegrating front lines there would be no way of containing the enemy. Slowly, German Panzer reinforcements struggled to the front, constantly harassed during the day by Allied fighter-bombers and slowed at night by French resistance fighters sabotaging roads, railway lines and rolling stock. First to arrive was *Brigadeführer* Werner Ostendorff's 17th *SS-Panzergrenadier* Division *Götz von Berlichingen*. It was followed by the *Wehrmacht's* 2nd *Panzer* Army which began to arrive, after a terrible journey, to reinforce the badly mauled *Panzer Lehr* Division.

RIGHT: *Reichsführer-SS* Heinrich Himmler pats a young boy on the cheek following a speech in 1944. Himmler was confident that his *Waffen-SS* troops would prove their worth during the Allied invasion of France, but ever since 6 June 1944 the Normandy battle had been in the process of wasting away one *SS* regiment after another. Like his beloved *Führer*, Himmler seemed deaf to any demands for withdrawal, and refused to believe reports of the enemy's strength and the exhaustion of the *SS* troops that were being flung from one overstretched sector to another. The *Waffen-SS* in the West in the summer of 1944 was on the point of being bled to death. But Himmler, the architect of the Imperial Guard of the Third Reich, was certain that his hand-picked body of Aryan supermen would win despite the odds against them. However, in spite of their fanatical courage and blind obedience to any order, the *Waffen-SS* were faced with too many Allied men, guns, tanks, fighters, bombers and naval guns to prevail.

ABOVE: A young *Hitlerjugend* soldier lays out a national flag for aerial recognition – a somewhat futile gesture, since Allied aircraft outnumbered the *Luftwaffe* more than fifty to one over the battlefront. But despite increasingly telling pressure, the 12th *SS-Panzer* Division carried on fighting superbly to hold its positions in the ruins around Caen. The young grenadiers did not expect to move very fast against the constant artillery shelling and naval bombardments. Instead, meticulously camouflaged, they were deployed in the ruins of houses, in ditches and alongside Panzers as mobile strongpoints. Caked in dust with the grime of battle over their unwashed faces they fought in the appalling heat against terrible odds. The tension was often so great that the tracks made by grenadiers going to and from their positions at night were frantically swept away before daylight brought spotter aircraft. But still, under the constant hammer blows of enemy artillery and anti-tank fire, Panzers of the 12th *SS* moved forward, supported by grenadiers.

ABOVE: Soldiers of the 12th *SS-Panzer* Division take cover during the extensive fighting in Normandy. In spite of the high levels of courage shown in combat by the teenagers of the *Hitlerjugend*, the division was on the edge of ultimate disaster. A divisional report revealed on 17 June: 'The enemy can achieve success exclusively by use of his incredible superiority in material…the fighting value of his infantry is minor. One of the major conditions for a successful defence and later

attack is effective suppression of the enemy artillery…' By 24 June the losses to the division amounted to 2,550 men. For a number of days the division had been preparing new defences to prevent a suspected enemy offensive on the city of Caen. Foxholes were dug, positions for infantry and machine gun emplacements were set up in houses. Hundreds of defensive positions had been carefully selected, camouflaged and well-prepared for close combat.

RIGHT: *Waffen-SS* troops climb out of one of the many craters caused by British naval shelling in Normandy. Naval bombardment was a constant threat to the German forces. On 14 June 1944 the 12th *SS* divisional command post in Venoix near Caen came under direct naval shelling by British ships. The commander, *Brigadeführer* Fritz Witt, ordered everyone to take cover in a shelter. Being the last man to jump into the trench, he was still exposed when a shell exploded in the treetops and a hail of large fragments of shrapnel ripped into his head, killing him instantly. *Standartenführer* Kurt Meyer, commander of *Panzergrenadier* Regiment 25, was ordered to take command of the division: at only 33, 'Panzer' Meyer became the youngest divisional commander in the German armed forces.

RIGHT: A group of heavily camouflaged grenadiers from the 12th *SS-Panzer* Division move through a Normandy wood during 'Operation Epsom' in late June 1944. General Montgomery's armoured offensive was intended to break the deadlock in front of Caen. Up to that point, the campaign had been one of attrition, with the Germans giving better than they received. But the Germans could only reinforce their fighting troops with difficulty, while the Allies could make good any losses relatively quickly. From the middle of June, Montgomery began to marshal his forces for a major assault on Caen. 'Operation Epsom' was a bitterly fought battle. Dead soldiers and damaged equipment littered the battlefield as far as the eye could see. Little mercy was shown or expected. The Allies, endeavouring to expand their beachhead, became increasingly incensed at the conduct of the *Hitlerjugend* troopers, who fought so tenaciously against overwhelming odds. The problem was not so much their bravery as the fact that, like so many *SS* units, they were prone to atrocity. On 8 June, members of the 12th *SS* shot 45 Canadian prisoners captured at Authie. Over the next week the young *SS* fanatics murdered another 60 British and Canadian prisoners. In the same period, however, they lost more than 900 men killed in combat.

BELOW LEFT: *Waffen-SS* troops in the thick of battle against British forces during 'Operation Epsom'. As the battle began on 26 June, the 12th *SS-Panzer* divisional commander wrote: 'The morning is already dawning. Everything is still quiet. I am still near Rauray with Max Wünsche and watch the last Panzers roll into the assembly area…. Then the German batteries began firing barrages. The English low-level attack aircraft roar above and send their rockets howling into Rauray. The hell of the battle of material has begun. The first Panzers are rattling to the front. The attack initially advances well, but is stalled by an English counterattack. It turns into a battle of tank against tank, which was fought with great determination…. Caen is the objective of the attack. The city is to be throttled by a pincer attack. Caen is to be Montgomery's prize and will bring down the German front.' During the day's fighting, at least 50 British tanks were knocked out by Panzers and Paks alone. But the Panzergrenadiers took a heavy battering, and in some areas a number of battalions were totally wiped out. *Sturmmann* Jochem Leykauff wrote about the desperate battle with the British during the attack on Caen: 'The position can no longer be held. Grenadiers cling to the rocky trench. Mortar shells explode in the treetops. Heavy machine guns saw through the position. We grenadiers have no heavy weapons. We cling to our carbines….'

ABOVE: Three soldiers pass a burning farm near Caen in July 1944, probably during 'Operation Charnwood'. This began on 7 July with a preparatory bombardment of the city. The 406mm (16in) guns of the battleship HMS *Rodney* battered Caen, followed by a major RAF heavy bomber attack. On the morning of 8 July a major Allied attack on the city and surrounding areas was finally unleashed. In two days of desperate fighting some of the British infantry battalions had suffered 25 percent casualties. In the surrounding towns and villages the *Hitlerjugend* Division fought to the grim death to hold on and prevent the enemy from gaining ground. But by now the *Hitlerjugend* was not the only *SS-Panzer* division in the field: reinforcements for the Normandy front were arriving from all over Europe. Not the least of these was the senior *Waffen-SS* formation, the 1st *SS-Panzer Division Leibstandarte SS Adolf Hitler*.

LEFT: Fighting in the Caen sector was a bloody battle of attrition. The Germans, honed as they were by years of combat in the East, were much better man for man than their inexperienced opponents. But Allied numerical superiority began to tell, and it looked as though the 12th SS would be encircled and annihilated. But Hitler ordered that the Caen sector be held at all costs. *Panzer* Meyer was astonished by the '*Führer* Order' and contemplated ignoring it rather than watch his 'lads' commit divisional suicide. There were no more reserves, ammunition was rapidly running out, and the only course he had left was to be driven back by the enemy. Contrary to Hitler's orders the division's survivors were ordered to withdraw their heavy weapons from Caen, and take up new defensive positions in the rear. As they fell back the advancing Canadians rolled through their old positions.

ABOVE: A *Waffen-SS* machine-gun team opens fire. The weapon they are using is a Czech-built ZB-30, one of the finest weapons of its type, on which the British based their famous Bren gun. The reason the *Waffen-SS* used such weapons dated back to the early years of the organisation's existence. The German Army controlled weapons procurement before the war, and it was reluctant to hand out modern weapons to the Nazi Party's private army. The *SS* had to look for weapons elsewhere. Fortunately, the occupation of Bohemia and Moravia gave Germany access to the long-established and highly influential Czech arms industry, from which the *SS* acquired the ZB-30. As with all *SS* grenadiers, these troopers have taken great pains to deploy their weapons in the most advantageous defensive positions possible. With their elaborate camouflage smocks they blended well with the natural surroundings, and were very difficult to detect. In Normandy, *Waffen-SS* machine-gunners deployed a number of elaborate fallback defensive positions, allowing them to keep fighting even after being forced backwards by the enemy.

ABOVE: A Horch light truck in Normandy has been draped with foliage in order to conceal it from aerial attack. German vehicle losses in France in 1944 were catastrophic. By the end of the campaign, the bulk of *Waffen-SS* armoured vehicles, guns and equipment had been destroyed. The heaviest losses occurred in August 1944, by the end of which no front-line Panzer division could call on more than a handful of tanks and artillery pieces. Many drivers were terrified at the prospect of moving their vehicles during daylight hours through the Norman countryside, since that was when they were most vulnerable to Allied fighter-bomber attack. To avoid the worst of the losses, units were compelled to camouflage their vehicles and hole up during the day, only daring to move under the cover of darkness.

ABOVE: A motorcycle unit belonging to the *Das Reich* Division seen during its arduous drive from southern France to the Normandy sector. On 8 June 1944, some 15,000 *Das Reich* soldiers with 209 Panzers and self-propelled guns began pulling out of the town of Montauban. Ahead lay a 450-mile (720-km) march through France. The division's march was bathed in blood. *Das Reich*, which had originally driven through this area as the *SS-VT* division back in 1940, was subject to continual resistance attacks. To the tough *SS* men, who had spent many months in murderous combat with partisans in the East, the only response was in kind. *Das Reich*'s march left a trail of savage reprisals that included some of the most appalling atrocities committed in the West – though they were considered standard practice in the East.

ABOVE: A *Hitlerjugend* grenadier dismounts from his well-concealed Sd.Kfz 251 halftrack. Even after the British and Canadians finally reached Caen, pockets of resistance continued to hold out to the north and west, but by the late afternoon of 9 July 1944 the fighting was all but over. 'Panzer' Meyer wrote: 'The soldiers of 12th *SS-Panzer* Division were at the end of their physical endurance. They had fought at the front line for four weeks without any relief and suffered the mighty hammer blows of the battle.... They marched into battle with fresh, glowing faces. Today, mud-covered steel helmets threw their shadows on sunken faces whose eyes had seen the beyond all too often'. By 11 July the 12th *SS* were finally relieved by the *Leibstandarte*. The division had suffered 60 percent casualties, a third of whom were killed. Pulled back to Sassy and Bons, the survivors' rest and recuperation did not last long: they were in action a week later helping to stem the tide of another British offensive as Montgomery launched an attack to the east of Caen.

LEFT: A grenadier belonging to the 12th *SS-Panzer* Division *Hitlerjugend* seen during operations in Normandy. The soldier has draped foliage over his Sd.Kfz 251 halftrack to help camouflage it from possible ground or air attack. This photograph was taken in the Vimont sector in late July or early August 1944, where the 12th *SS-Panzer* Division was fighting a defensive action. All over the German front massive Allied bombing raids continued with unabated ferocity, pulverising troops and armoured columns alike. During this critical period the *Waffen-SS* tried its best to hold on to its positions, fighting a number of fierce local battles amid a heavy cacophony of artillery and tank fire. By early August conditions took a serious turn for the worse when the threatened American breakout took place. The Germans were now in danger of being encircled by the fast-moving American tank columns of Patton's Third US Army.

BELOW: A well-concealed machine-gunner watches some of his comrades returning after a reconnaissance patrol. The MG42 is mounted on a tripod and carries a sustained fire sight. All of the grenadiers are armed with the MP40 sub-machine gun. They are all wearing the second-type smock with full green 'oak leaf' on a red-brown background pattern, worn summer side out. Hooked to their Y-straps are their webbing assault packs. These consist of an A-frame to which are attached mess tin, gasmask canister with gas cape bag, and rolled *Zeltbahn* strapped round the outside. Hanging from their belts are the bread bag, water bottle, entrenching tool and magazine pouches for their MP40 sub-machine gun.

ABOVE: A soldier belonging to the 716th Infantry Division emerging from one of the defensive positions set up on the Normandy coast in 1944. Prior to the Allied invasion of Normandy, *Brigadeführer* Fritz Witt, commander of the 12th *SS-Panzer* Division, drove out to the Channel coast in order to gather information on areas into which his division was likely to deploy. Witt was not impressed: he considered that the 716th Infantry Division's positions along the beach were far from adequate. Behind the artillery bunkers and heavy machine-gun positions were a small number of anti-tank weapons. Many of the bunkers were still under construction, and even those that were still being built lacked protection from aerial attacks or naval gunfire. Given the state of the defences, Witt was convinced that the Allies would land successfully, and with the expected bombardment from sea and air he was sure that the enemy would quickly advance inland. After making an intensive examination of the roads and bridges leading out of the coastal area, Witt was convinced that the sector around the ancient city of Caen was particularly tempting for the enemy advance. Witt was sure that Caen would become a major focus for combat after any landing on the Normandy coast. However, Witt's fears were not shared by the German High Command, which was wrongly convinced that the most likely location for an Allied invasion was the Pas de Calais. Even if the British and Americans did land in Normandy, it would only be a feint to draw attention away from the north.

BELOW: An armoured unit belonging to the *Das Reich* Division just prior to entering the Normandy sector. A Horch field car, more than likely serving as a temporary command post, has been heavily camouflaged with straw to minimise the increasing risk of aerial attack. The closer *Das Reich* got to Normandy, the more its units had to travel by night. As they entered the Norman countryside, drivers inched their vehicles painfully forward, occasionally leaping from their trucks or armoured vehicles to seek cover beneath the hulls of tanks as aircraft swooped into attack. Virtually all the *Das Reich* armoured units that arrived in Normandy were in such bad shape that they needed days to regroup before going into action. German

Panzer commanders made increasingly desperate requests for fuel, replacements, new routings and other important materials needed to sustain their drive. The division arrived exhausted in the rear areas of the battle zone between 15 and 30 June, nearly three weeks behind schedule. *Das Reich* did not enter combat until early July, by which time it had already suffered heavy losses. Units were fed piecemeal into battle with the Americans at Coutances, St Lô, Percy and Mortain. Despite its severe mauling by Allied bombing, the division was far from beaten. But its reputation would now forever be associated with the terrible atrocities it unleashed during its 450-mile (720-km) march through France.

RIGHT: Inside a freshly dug foxhole, a well-camou-flaged grenadier attached to the 12th *SS-Panzer* Division *Hitlerjugend* is about to survey the terrain through his dark yellow 6 x 30 binoculars. Note the M24 stick grenade lying to one side. This photograph was taken during vicious fighting in what became known as the Falaise pocket. In July 1944 the 12th *SS* was pulled out of the Normandy front, but as German positions between Maltot and Vendes threatened to collapse, the *Hitlerjugend* division was once again thrown back into the thick of action. Here, many of the *Waffen-SS* soldiers perished. Those elements that were not massacred or captured in the huge encir-clement only managed to break out by leaving the bulk of their equipment behind. The *Hitlerjugend* had been sent to Normandy to prove themselves in battle, but for all too many of the young believers in the *Führer*, Normandy was not only their testing ground, but was also their grave. Many hundreds more were killed as German forces fought their way back towards the borders of the Reich, chased by fast-moving Allied armour. By the end of August 1944, the battle of Normandy was over. The 12th *SS* had become a shadow of the formation that had moved so confi-dently into battle some ten weeks before. When it retreated across the Meuse near Yvoir in early September, it consisted of only 600 men, with all its tanks gone and no ammunition for the artillery. Field

Marshal von Rundstedt was saddened at the state of the *Hitlerjugend* Division and remarked that it was: 'a pity that this faithful youth is sacrificed in a hope-less situation'. Following its virtual annihilation in Normandy, the division fought a series of minor holding actions as it withdrew from France into Belgium. By mid-September 1944, the exhausted 12th *SS-Panzer* Division had been transferred back to Germany for refitting so that it could participate in the Ardennes offensive.

LEFT: A StuG III Ausf.G on a dusty track somewhere in northern France in August 1944. It was a year earlier, in 1943, that this final StuG III variant entered service. It mounted a lethal 7.5cm (2.95in) StuK 40 L/48 gun that delivered enhanced armour penetration of up to 91mm (3.6in) of 30-degree sloped armour, and 109mm (4.3in) of unsloped armour at 1,000m (1,094yds). For close-in defence the vehicle was also equipped with a 7.92mm (0.31in) MG34 machine gun. During the spring of 1944 the *Waffen-SS* were assigned two companies each of 22 StuG III Ausf.G assault guns, which were attached to the Panzer regi-ments of the *Das Reich* and *Leibstandarte* Divisions, in preparation for the expected Allied invasion of France. During the battles in Normandy *SS* grenadiers relied heavily on fire support from the StuG III, which was at its best fighting from defensive positions against advancing enemy armoured formations.

LEFT: An *SS* grenadier belonging to the 9th *SS-Panzer* Division *Hohenstaufen* poses for the camera in an impressed civilian vehicle which has been painted in a camouflage scheme. Based in Poland on 6 June, *Hohenstaufen* together with the 10th *SS-Panzer* Division *Frundsberg* was immediately ordered to the battlefront. The devastation wrought by Allied attacks meant that it took the two divisions longer to cross France than it had taken them to cross the rest of Europe. On 3 August 1944 *Hohenstaufen* attempted to smash advanced British forces attacks between Chenedolle and Montchamp. But because the division had been severely weakened by constant Allied aerial and ground attacks, it could only achieve a partial success. The 10th *SS-Panzer* Division *Frundsberg* disengaged from the Aunay sector and started to support units of *Hohenstaufen* as it began making more determined strikes against the town of Chenedolle. The battle for the actual town was fought between 4 and 7 August, ending when the two *Waffen-SS* units disengaged and withdrew from the area.

ABOVE: On the retreat across the Seine an unidentified unit belonging to the 12th *SS-Panzer* Division *Hitlerjugend* use parts of a damaged bridge in order to move a BMW motorcycle combination past an obstacle. During the night of 24-25 August 1944 the last part of the *Hitlerjugend Kampfgruppe* Mohnke, crossed the Seine, almost spelling the end of the division's deployment in France. On 25 August, the supreme command of the 5th *Panzer* Army finally ordered all of its units fighting south of the river, to withdraw behind the Risle and Seine. As the last units withdrew strong defensive positions were constructed in order to allow all the remaining *Hitlerjugend* grenadiers to cross safely without being severely harassed by the enemy. By the morning of 26 August the bulk of the 12th *SS-Division* was behind the Seine in the sector Amfreville-sous-les-Monts-Muids, while other units moved west of Beaumont. The mass of the grenadiers assembled in the Beauvais area with stragglers from the division arriving daily through the last days of August and early September. Some of these stragglers had been left behind in Normandy, and had made their own way to safety through enemy held territory. A number had discarded their distinctive *Waffen-SS* camouflage uniforms and had made their way through the French countryside dressed in farmer's clothes, with milk containers, rakes and pitchforks. Others were dressed as mourners with wreaths.

LEFT: One of the most feared tanks in Normandy, a Pz.Kpfw.VI Tiger I Ausf.E. The Tiger tank was slow, lacked range, and its turret was very sluggish to traverse, but its thick armour and powerful gun meant that in capable hands it could dominate a battlefield. The Tiger was never available in large numbers, and the two *SS* heavy tank battalions in Normandy had no more than 90 Tigers on strength. But those few tanks inflicted damage out of all proportion to their numbers. Indeed, Tiger ace Michael Wittman and his crew managed to stop the attack of an entire British division at Villers-Bocage. The sheer power of the Tiger, together with the vast combat experience of its crews, filled Allied tankmen with dread. The problem of 'Tiger-phobia' became so bad that General Montgomery was forced to step in, banning the distribution of reports of Tiger actions which showed Allied tankers in a very unfavourable light.

RIGHT: A *Waffen-SS* Pz.Kpfw.V Panther Ausf.G advances through a destroyed French town in late July 1944. The Panther was armed with a long-barrelled, high-velocity KwK 42 L/70 7.5cm (2.95in) gun and had two 7.92mm (0.31in) MG34 machine guns for defence against infantry. The tank weighed 44.8 tonnes (44 tons) and was powered by 700bhp Maybach HL 230 P30 V12-cylinder petrol engine. It had a maximum road speed of 46kph (29mph) and a maximum cross-country speed of 30kph (19mph). Prior to the Allied invasion of Normandy the *Waffen-SS* went through a major transition with *SS* Panzer divisions receiving an entire battalion of Panther tanks. Apart from the *Totenkopf* and the 5th *SS-Panzer* Division *Wiking* that remained on the Eastern Front, the *Leibstandarte*, *Das Reich*, *Hitlerjugend*, *Hohenstaufen* and *Frundsberg* were all given Panthers for operations in the West. A normal *Waffen-SS* Panther battalion fielded 76 Panther V tanks; four companies each with 17 tanks and a headquarters company with another eight Panthers. The Panzer regiment staff company had a further three command Panthers that brought nominal battalion strength up to 79 Panthers, including six command tanks. However, by the time the Allies unleashed their assault into France in June 1944 most of the *Waffen-SS* Panther battalions had less than half their authorised strength. One division, however, that was well equipped with the Panther was the 12th *SS-Panzer*

Division *Hitlerjugend*. By the time D-Day began, the *Hitlerjugend* had 81 Panthers on strength, consisting mainly of Ausf.G models. The Panther was possibly the best all-round tank of the war, having a powerful gun and excellent sloped armour. Originally designed in response to the superb Soviet T-34, the Panther made its combat debut at Kursk in 1943, and it remained in production to the end of the war. But it was complex and expensive to build. Total production of the Panther was just over 5,000 – compared to more than 11,000 Soviet T-34s built in 1944 alone.

RIGHT: A member of the *Leibstandarte* division poses on an Sd.Kfz.251 half-track during operations in France in early August 1944. Note the divisional insignia of the 1st *SS-Panzer* Division painted in white on the right front of the vehicle. The key symbol is a play on the name of Sepp Dietrich, the *Leibstandarte's* original commander. 'Dietrich' is a German slang term for a skeleton key, hence the symbol. On the left-hand side, also painted in white, is the Panzergrenadier tactical sign denoting the unit to which this vehicle was assigned. Prior to the Allied invasion of Normandy, the *Leibstandarte* had been encamped in the area of Bruges in Belgium, but it was kept in reserve and was not called into action until eleven days after D-Day. The division concentrated its forces at Caen, and it soon became embroiled in heavy combat. It was later moved across the battlefield to the American sector, where it was to take part in the over-ambitious and ultimately futile Mortain counter attack. On 7 August, the division was badly mauled by rocket-firing RAF Typhoons, and on 16 August the High Command ordered a withdrawal.

LEFT: A *Waffen-SS Wespe* crew in action. This self-propelled howitzer was armed with a 10.5cm (4.1in) leFH 18/2 L/28 field howitzer mounted in a thinly armoured, open-topped box structure-built on top of a Pz.Kpfw.II light tank chassis. It was powered by a 140bhp Maybach HL 62 TR R6–cylinder petrol engine. It had a maximum cross-country speed of 20kph (12.5mph). These vehicles served in the armoured artillery battalions of the *SS* Panzer divisions. Each battalion comprised two light batteries of six *Wespe* vehicles and one heavy battery equipped with six heavier *Hummels*.

ABOVE: An artillery crew belonging to the 12th *SS-Panzer* Division *Hitlerjugend* fires against an advancing British or American target during the last phases of the French campaign, taking place in August 1944. These soldiers are more than likely fighting a desperate rearguard action in northern France, and when they fire their last rounds will have to try to escape on foot, leaving their artillery piece behind. In spite of the dishevelled and exhausted appearance of many of the soldiers who withdrew across the French border into Belgium and Germany, they were the survivors of three months of constant battle, and their experience would prove to be invaluable when the divisions were reconstituted. Although now filled with unwilling conscripts, the rebuilt *SS* divisions still maintained the *SS* tradition of combat success. But above average fighting ability was not just an *SS* phenomenon. All through the war, the German soldier consistently outperformed his Allied counterparts. It was partly a function of training – German soldiers were expected to show initiative, and all soldiers were trained to function at least three ranks higher than their actual position. Shoot the officers of a German unit, and the sergeants took over. Do the same to a British unit and the instinctive reaction was to retreat to a defensive position and wait for orders.

ABOVE: A *Das Reich* Flak crewman scans the French skies on the edge of the Falaise Pocket. He is standing on the fighting platform of a 2cm (0.78in) *Flakvierling* 38 quadruple-barrelled self-propelled anti-aircraft gun mounted on the back of a halftrack artillery tractor. *Das Reich* fought in Normandy as it had done on the Eastern Front so many times before. When called to task for committing atrocities, one *Das Reich* officer was genuinely puzzled, since killing prisoners had been standard practice in the two years he had served on the Eastern Front. In August the division received orders to join the II *SS-Panzer* Corps and move to Vimoutiers, a town located several miles outside the Falaise Pocket. It was in this area that the men of *Das Reich* were to maintain a strong presence and ensure that the German Armies had an escape route out of the pocket. When the Allies eventually sealed the Falaise Pocket with 15 German divisions trapped inside, it was the task of the *Das Reich* Division to try to force open and hold a corridor which would provide surviving German units and individuals with an escape route. Thanks to a communications breakdown between the Allied armies, the trap was not sealed tight, and tens of thousands of German soldiers escaped through the gap held open by the *SS*. However, hundreds of thousands did not escape the catastrophe.

BELOW: An assault gun battalion belonging to the *Leibstandarte* advances through a French town at dawn. Heading towards the front, it is nervously aware of Allied bombers in the area. These StuG III Ausf.Gs have received a coating of anti-magnetic mine paste, but as yet no attempt has been made to camouflage the vehicles. Few who had not encountered it could imagine the full impact of Allied superiority in the air. Only those troops who had served at the end of the North African campaign would realize just how deadly tactical aircraft could be. On 22 August 1944 Army Group B issued a report and noted the strengths of the eight surviving Panzer divisions that took part in the battle for Normandy. The *Leibstandarte* was typical; it had suffered terrible losses and the once powerful *SS* Panzer Division was now no more than a weak battalion – all of its tanks were lost and its artillery was almost non-existent.

LEFT: *Waffen-SS* Panzergrenadiers advance with an Sd.Kfz.251 halftrack during operations in northern France in late August 1944. The halftrack appears to have camouflage netting draped over part of the crew compartment. Such netting was used extensively by Panzer and assault gun crews in France. Of interest is the grenadier armed with an MG42 machine gun. Behind the machine gunner is a soldier carrying the *Lafette* 42 tripod on his back. When set up for sustained firing on fixed lines the MG42 machine gun was mounted on the *Lafette* tripod where it could be remotely fired from the rear by use of a trigger close to the traversing and elevating controls.

ABOVE: A 2cm (0.78in) Flak 38 self-propelled anti air-craft gun mounted on the back of a halftrack artillery tractor is seen in action in the later stages of the battle of France. During the second half of August *Waffen-SS* formations began an agonising withdrawal through France. In the Falaise region the *Das Reich*, *Hohenstaufen* and remnants of the *Hitlerjugend* divisions launched a series of heavy counterattacks in order to relieve German divisions trapped inside the Falaise Pocket. Although the *Waffen-SS* managed to punch a hole to allow their comrades to escape the impending slaughter, losses in and around Falaise were massive. By the end of August 1944 the first part of the campaign in the West had been lost by Germany. It had been a very costly battle, with many highly effective units being virtually annihilated. Although the average *SS* grenadier proved capable of meeting the highest standards, fighting courageously with self-sacrifice against massive numerical and material superiority, he could only delay the enemy, not defeat him.

LEFT: Grenadiers belonging to an unidentified *Waffen-SS* division seen during its withdrawal through Normandy following its almost total annihilation in the area. By the end August 1944 the *Waffen-SS* was a shadow of its former self. The *Das Reich* Division had experienced a terrible mauling and had only 15 tanks and some 450 men remaining. The *Hohenstaufen* Division fared only slightly better, with some 25 tanks and 460 men surviving; the *Frundsberg* had all its tanks obliterated and all its artillery destroyed, and was now just four battalions of infantry; and the *Hitlerjugend* had 10 tanks and no artillery with just 300 men. Its *Wehrmacht* counterparts also suffered; 2nd *Panzer* Division had lost all of its tanks and guns; the elite *Panzer Lehr* Division had been totally obliter-ated and no longer existed as a cohesive unit.

ABOVE: A Pz.Kpfw Tiger IV Ausf.E of *Schwere SS-Panzer-Abteilung 101* in Normandy. Special features were introduced to this Tiger in December 1943 and January 1944 and consisted of a cut-out hull side extension which allowed free movement for the shackle, the smaller muzzlebrake, the chevron faced track and the centre mounted Bosch headlight. This particular Tiger more than likely has steel rimmed wheels that were delivered to the *sSS-PzAbt. 101* in April 1944. All the external vertical surfaces of the Tiger are coated in *Zimmerit* anti-magnetic paste and the whole vehicle is painted in dark yellow. It was the crew that most probably applied the dark green and red brown camouflage stripes. Note the unit insignia, crossed keys in a shield surrounded by oak leaves, painted in white on the front right side of the armour.

The *sSS-PzAbt.101* saw extensive action in the Normandy sector; this included the Tigers of *Obersturmführer* Michael Wittmann's 2nd Company that inflicted massive casualties against British armoured units. By the time of his death on 8 August 1944, Wittmann, now promoted *SS-Hauptsturm-führer*, had become the most successful tank ace of the war, and possibly of all time. By the time he was posted to France, his personal score exceeded 117 tank kills. His solo attack at Villers-Bocage brought a probing attack by the 7th Armoured Division to a halt: in a matter of minutes, Wittmann's Tiger accounted for 25 British tanks, 14 half-tracks and 14 Bren gun carriers. His skill and tenacity earned him the highly coveted Knight's Cross-with Oak Leaves and Swords. He died later in the campaign.

ABOVE: One of the 90 Tiger tanks belonging to the *Waffen-SS* Panzer divisions destroyed during the battle for Normandy. This Tiger is one of many armoured vehicles that were trapped and eventually knocked out inside the Falaise Pocket. By mid August, there were five *SS* Panzer divisions, six Army Panzer divisions, and eight infantry divisions caught in the pocket

RIGHT: A Pz.Kpfw.VI Tiger I Ausf.E halted on a road. The Tiger tank was a fearsome vehicle to British and American tankers in Normandy. Its thick frontal armour meant that the only Allied tank with a chance of taking out a Tiger was the Sherman Firefly – an M4 Sherman fitted with a powerful British 17-pdr anti-tank gun. However, the Germans soon recognized the threat, and long-barrelled Shermans were priority targets for all Panzer crews. Otherwise, standard practice by Allied tank crews was to 'engage a Tiger or a Panther with at least five tanks – and expect to lose three or four of them'. Big and powerful though the Tiger was, it was about to be superseded by an even bigger tank, the Tiger II or King Tiger. Heavier, with thicker sloped armour, the Tiger II was armed with an upgraded 8.8cm (3.45in) gun with a higher muzzle velocity than the original. King Tigers were sent for

between the US Third Army and the Canadian First Army. German armoured formations – especially the 12th *SS-Panzer* Division – kept the jaws of the pincers open long enough to avert a total catastrophe. By 20 August 1944, the Allied pincers met and the pocket was sealed. Some 50,000 prisoners were captured with over 10,000 dead on the battlefield.

trials in Normandy, but they saw their most extensive use with the *SS* in the Ardennes and in the final battles against the Red Army in Hungary.

BELOW: A group of what appear to be *SS* Pz.Kpfw.V Panther Ausf.Gs in a Norman village. Of interest is how the Panther crews have gone to great lengths to camouflage their vehicles by applying plenty of foliage. They are camouflaged in this way in order to avoid detection from Allied fighters. By this period of the campaign in the West Panzer losses were massive. All the key *Waffen-SS* divisions had been reduced to a handful of tanks and artillery pieces by August 1944. Nevertheless, in spite of Allied numerical superiority, the Panther enjoyed some success in combat with Allied tank forces. During the last weeks of the Normandy battle the Germans successfully utilised their armoured Panther battle groups to temporarily halt the enemy, despite the huge losses that were consequently inflicted upon them. From 14 August 1944, remnants of the *Waffen-SS* Panther groups conducted a fighting withdrawal in the face of increasing opposition. On 19 August, the *SS* launched the few remaining Panthers of the II *SS-Panzer* Corps from outside the Falaise Pocket in an attempt to smash an escape route to the encircled German formations. Although in very small numbers the Panther showed

its worth and *SS* tank crews managed to prize open a gap and allow the remaining German units to escape from the hell of Falaise. Precious little equipment escaped from the inferno. The *Das Reich* Division was one such elite formation that failed to remove a single working Panther from the pocket. However, at least 36 Panthers did escape, but most succumbed to Allied air attacks as the Panther battle groups withdrew towards the Seine. Both day and night armoured vehicles and weary infantrymen withdrew across the river ahead of the advancing Allies. By the time the Allies raced across the Seine, there were no more than 15 Panthers in the West. The German armoured formations of the *Westheer* now ceased to exist, and it seemed that nothing could prevent the Allies as they spearheaded through France, into Belgium and on to the very frontiers of the German homeland. However, just one month later the remnants of two *SS* Panzer divisions would smash Montgomery's operation at Arnhem, and three months later the survivors of Normandy would provide the core of three entire armies scraped together to make an assault through the Ardennes.

ARDENNES OFFENSIVE

Late in September 1944 Hitler planned a massive offensive through the Belgian Ardennes, which he thought would alter the course of the war.

He issued these secret orders to Ob. West – the headquarters of the Commander-in-Chief for the Western Front. I *SS-Panzer* Corps with the 1st and 12th *SS-Panzer* Division, and II *SS-Panzer* Corps with the 2nd and 9th *SS-Panzer* Divisions, were to be released for reorganisation and training; the *Panzer Lehr* Division was also to be reformed and released for this decisive battle.

Three of the four armies in *Generalfeldmarschall* Walter Model's Army Group B were slated to play the major role in the offensive. These were *SS-Oberstgruppenführer* 'Sepp' Dietrich's Sixth *SS-Panzer* Army, *General der Panzertruppen* Hasso von Manteuffel's Fifth *Panzer* Army, and *General der Panzertruppen* Erich Brandenberger's Seventh Army. All units were reinforced and prepared for action.

LEFT: A *Waffen-SS* anti-tank team armed with an old 3.7cm (1.45in) Pak 35/36 stands ready for action during the Ardennes offensive in December 1944. Ever since the catastrophic defeat in Normandy, Hitler had been searching for an opportunity to regain the initiative in the West. He told his commanders to launch a great winter counter-attack through the Ardennes – scene of his 1940 victory – to capture the port of Antwerp.

At this point in the war, German Panzer divisions had one Panzer and two *Panzergrenadier* regiments. The divisions averaged about 100 medium tanks. Overall the Germans amazingly collected over 1,000 Panzers and assault gun vehicles for the Ardennes offensive.

The code name for the offensive was *Wacht am Rhein* or 'Watch on the Rhine'. The plan called for a three-pronged assault towards Antwerp. Its main strike component, the Sixth *SS-Panzer* Army, was to attack through the Ardennes forests and force a crossing of the River Meuse between Liege and Huy, before driving on the massive Allied supply base at Antwerp.

Capturing the bridges over the Meuse was the mission of a specially created force called *Panzerbrigade* 150, commanded by *SS-Sturmbannführer* Otto Skorzeny. Dressed in American military police uniforms and issued with American weapons and vehicles, these English-speaking volunteers were to mingle with retreating American troops with the sole intention of spreading fear and confusion among the enemy ranks. Behind this special force the I *SS-Panzer* Corps, would punch its way through American lines.

On the morning of 16 December 1944, the dawn quiet was shattered by 2,000 light, medium, and heavy guns, howitzers, and multiple-rocket launchers, opening fire simultaneously. But as abruptly as the bombardment began, it ended, leaving a stunned silence. Then from beneath the pines and camouflage netting thousands of *Wehrmacht* and *Waffen-SS* soldiers began their offensive. All along the German line, from the Sixth *SS-Panzer* Army in the north to the Seventh Army in the south, a massive collection of troops and armour crashed into action through the freezing morning fog. The speed and depth of the German attack was a brilliant coordinated display of all arms cooperation.

For the second line American divisions manning this supposedly quiet sector, the attack came as a total surprise. They had been told that the Germans were finished, and that victory was just around the corner. Now they were being hit hard by veteran *Waffen-SS* units with the latest German armour at their disposal. The green American units were quickly bundled out of their forward positions and began retreating to the west.

A few miles north of St Vith, in the village of Manderfeld, American troops were receiving a hammering. They were being attacked by the grenadiers of the 18th *Volksgrenadier* Division, and by the advanced guard of *Kampfgruppe* Peiper, the spearhead of the *1st SS-Panzer* Division *Leibstandarte Adolf Hitler*. Peiper had been a ruthless *SS* commander on the Eastern Front, and now this same ruthlessness was also to mark the march of his *Kampfgruppe* across the Ardennes.

Field Marshal von Rundstedt said: 'Antwerp? If we get as far as the Meuse we should get down on our knees and thank God!'

The *SS Kampfgruppe* bulldozed its way past Manderfeld with American troops quickly taking to their heels. In the town of Honsfeld Peiper's Panthers moved into the streets. Almost immediately *SS* troops began their trail of massacres by murdering 19 American soldiers who had surrendered. On the same day at a crossroads near Malmedy, 125 prisoners were rounded up, herded into a snowy field and shot.

To the south in the Seventh Army sector, the 902nd *Panzergrenadier* Regiment of the *Panzer Lehr* Division was approaching Bastogne, whose defenders had been reinforced by the American 101st Airborne Division. The capture of Bastogne was essential to the successful development of their offensive. During the night of 18-19 December two German Panzer divisions arrived, and by the following day the town was almost completely surrounded.

On the morning of 22 December more German troops and armour arrived ready for action. As they poised to attack later that day *Oberleutnant* Helmuth Henke, of *Panzer Lehr* Division's operations section, carried demands for 'the honourable surrender of the town' to the American commander, only to receive the classic reply 'Nuts!'. They would never give up the town to the Germans. The fighting for Bastogne continued.

On 23 December the Germans mounted their main assault with a series of heavy multi-pronged attacks against the American perimeter. Both sides sufferd huge losses, but the Americans were resolute in defending the town and preventing *Panzer Lehr* Division's infantry from gaining ground. On Christmas day the fighting continued with unabated ferocity. Around the smouldering town American tanks, halftracks and advancing infantry moved into action. Almost at once the Germans, who by now included units of *Volksgrenadier*, *Fallschirmjäger*, *Wehrmacht* and *Waffen-SS* came out to meet them. Guns, bayonets, knives and grenades were used as German grenadiers and American armoured infantry became locked in a desperate battle of attrition.

For the next week fighting continued to rage. On 30 December the fighting had become so intense that the *Leibstandarte* reported it had lost about thirty Panzers and many of its grenadiers. Up above Allied fighters dominated the sky and attacked any German vehicle or movement on the roads and open fields. As a consequence *Waffen-SS* units suffered huge casualties. Slowly, with additional support by the British XXX Corps, the Germans were reluctantly forced on the defensive and driven back, this time for good. Nearly 12,000 German soldiers had been killed attempting to capture the town and 900 Americans died defending it, with another 3,000 killed outside its perimeter. Altogether the Germans lost some 450 tanks during the battle.

All over the Ardennes German troops were exhausted. At night the soldiers watched from their freezing positions as bombers mounted a continuous aerial onslaught. The Allied bombing had caused widespread destruction in the Ardennes. Bridges were knocked out, roads were cratered and villages had been razed to the ground, forcing armoured columns on long detours. The incessant Allied air attacks, coupled with severe shortages of fuel and reserves, had finally ground the Ardennes offensive to a halt.

With so many Allied forces being employed in

ABOVE: For the attack in the Ardennes, the four armies of Field Marshal Walter Model's Army Group B, played the major role. The Fifteenth Army, however, was not to take part in the operation, but the three other armies in Model's army group were prepared for action. For this important offensive Hitler made sure that the SS divisions involved were of the highest quality. The newly refitted *SS Panzer* divisions *Leibstandarte*, *Das Reich*, *Hohenstaufen* and *Hitlerjugend* formed I and II *SS-Panzer* Corps of the Sixth *SS-Panzer* Army. It was the first time Germany had fielded an entire army composed of *Waffen-SS* troops.

the Ardennes, Hitler was slowly forced to realize how much was at stake in the west. On 8 January Hitler grudgingly ordered the forward units to fall back to a line that ran south from Dochamps, in the Samrée-Baraque de Fraiture area, to Longchamps, which was 8km (5 miles) north of Bastogne. Even more significant were orders for the mighty elite *SS Panzer* divisions to go over to the defensive. The Sixth *Panzer* Army was withdrawn into reserve under Hitler's personal command, and he also called back the remnants of his foremost fighting machine, the *Leibstandarte Adolf Hitler*, from Bastogne. Hitler quietly admitted that his *Wacht am Rhein* had moved towards its *Gotterdammerung*. The *Führer* had in fact postponed the Western Allies' advance into Germany by no more than five weeks. His last gamble, using some of the most powerful formations the *Wehrmacht* and *Waffen-SS* could scrape together, had failed. By the end of January 1945, the Germans were back to where they had started six weeks earlier.

ABOVE: An *SS* machine-gun team takes up a covering position during the Ardennes offensive. On 16 December 1944, in the village of Manderfeld a few miles north of St Vith, the American 14th Cavalry Group was under attack by the 18th *Volksgrenadier* Division and *Kampfgruppe* Peiper of the *Leibstandarte*. *Obersturmbannführer* Joachim 'Jochen' Peiper was a ruthless tank commander who drove his men through the Ardennes with absolute aggression. At his disposal he had about 100 Panzer IVs and Panthers, together with a heavy battalion of 42 Tigers. The 3rd

Battalion of the 2nd *SS-Panzergrenadier* Regiment, equipped with armoured self-propelled guns rather than tanks, provided Peiper's *Kampfgruppe* with strong motorized infantry support. Artillery fire, shells from tanks, mortar bombs and machine gun fire from Peiper's infantry turned Manderfeld into a cauldron of fire and smoke. Greatly outnumbered and outgunned, the inexperienced American soldiers quickly lost heart, and needed little or no encouragement to escape the bloodbath promised by some of the toughest and most ruthless fighting men in the whole of the *SS*.

LEFT: In a drastic attempt to prop up the dwindling German gains in the Ardennes, Hitler threw in additional forces and ordered the launching of a new offensive in Alsace. Intelligence reports indicated that American lines had been thinned in order to send reinforcements north to the Bulge. A mountain warfare instructor gives direction to two young soldiers just prior to action. Operation *Nordwind* was launched on 1 January 1945 with eight divisions, including the 17th *SS-Panzergrenadier* Division *Götz von Berlichingen*, the 6th *SS-Gebirgs* Division and the 10th *SS-Panzer* Division *Frundsberg*. It failed to achieve anything but massive losses of men and equipment.

ABOVE: A group of *Waffen-SS* troops fire at the besieged town of Bastogne. The men are armed with Kar 98K rifles and MP40 sub-machine guns, and one soldier can be seen changing a barrel to his MG34 machine-gun. Bastogne was the key junction in the road network through which the German forces were advancing, and both sides were well aware of its importance. The Americans knew that if Bastogne could be held, the chances of the Germans reaching the Meuse River would be seriously disrupted. In preparation for operations in the snow around Bastogne, most of the *Wehrmacht* and *Waffen-SS* troops painted their tanks and other vehicles in white, and their grenadiers dressed in white camouflage smocks. The fighting for the town was intense, with both sides suffering significant losses. However, before the siege had begun the defenders had been reinforced by the 'Screaming Eagles' of the 101st Airborne Division, and the elite paratroopers were enough to hold the Germans back. In a last desperate effort to smash into Bastogne, a powerful *Kampfgruppe* was formed from the weakened *Leibstandarte*, which had been brought down from the Sixth *Panzer* Army's front, and the 167th *Volksgrenadier* Division, which had recent combat experience on the Eastern Front. It was not enough: the Americans held on to Bastogne.

ABOVE: An *SS* motorcyclist in the Ardennes has halted on a road to check his position. Although the German offensive came as a complete surprise to the Allies and to the weak American forces holding the Ardennes sector of the front, the Germans never really had the resources – or the fuel – to exploit the situation. Hitler's grandiose plan to split the Allies and capture Antwerp was doomed to failure. The deepest penetration – some 96km (60 miles) – had been achieved by the 2nd *Panzer* Division, but it fell short of its main objective of the Meuse. *Kampfgruppe* Peiper, which had led the advance initially, had stalled against increasing Allied forces. Peiper's tanks and grenadiers had advanced no more than 48km (30 miles) before they became engaged in a series of battles in the area of La Gleize and Stoumont. Low on ammunition, out of fuel and facing Allied forces appearing on the battlefield in ever-increasing strength, Peiper's position deteriorated. By Christmas Eve the *SS* commander ordered the destruction of his remaining vehicles, then led his 800 surviving men on a long retreat, marching back to the start lines they had left such a short time before.

LEFT: An *SS* machine-gunner, wearing a white camouflage smock, covers advancing German infantrymen. A StuG.III Ausf.G assault gun can be seen in the distance. As fuel supplies drastically dwindled, it was the economical StuG III that the *SS* assault gun crews chose to keep operational. By this period of the war *SS* motorised infantry divisions needed more tanks than could be manufactured. Since the StuG was cheaper and quicker to build than a tank, many were deployed as tank substitutes. Although less versatile than turreted armour, the assault gun proved to be an effective weapon, especially during the early stages of the Ardennes offensive. Nevertheless, once fuel supplies ran out they became sitting ducks to Allied armour, tank-destroyers and bazooka-armed infantry.

BELOW: *SS Nebeltruppe* supporting the attack on Bastogne load a battery of halftrack mounted, 10-barrelled, 15cm (5.9in) *Panzerwerfer* 42 rocket launchers. Rockets were fearsome weapons, much used on the Eastern Front, and they added their distinctive sound to the final German attempt to take the town, launched at dawn on 30 December. Fierce, confused fighting went on all day with Americans calling in armour, fighter-bomber and heavy artillery support. During the battle, the *Leibstandarte* lost 30 tanks and the division's Panzergrenadiers took a severe hammering. As fighting continued into New Year, a German paratrooper noted: 'The enemy had offered the most bitter resistance and employed masses of artillery and armour. We suffered heavy losses. Above us enemy fighter-bombers and artillery-spotting aircraft clouded the skies. They attacked any vehicle or movement on the roads and open fields. Some of us took cover behind a house where we discovered injured men of the *Leibstandarte* were sheltering.'

ABOVE: One of the very few operational German tanks in the Ardennes is heavily camouflaged with branches and foliage after the failure of *Wacht am Rhein*. The camouflage was essential to protect the tank from Allied air attack. The first stages of the German offensive had been carried out in bad weather under cloudy skies, but when the weather cleared over the Ardennes on 23 December, Allied tactical aircraft flew more than 7,000 sorties in just four days. 'The attacks from the air,' wrote an *SS* officer, 'were so powerful that even single vehicles could only get through by going from cover to cover.' The tank is a Pz.Kpfw.IV Ausf.H armed with a long-barrelled 7.5cm (2.95in) gun. By the time this photo was taken, early in January 1945, it was the morale of the men rather than the shortage of armour which caused most concern. The remnants of the *Waffen-SS* units were exhausted from constant combat. The initial confidence generated by early success was lost as shortage of rations, lack of sleep and the constant Allied shelling and bombing drained their energy.

ABOVE: A battery of *Wespe* (Wasp) self-propelled guns, hastily transferred from the Eastern Front in an attempt to prop up the disintegrating German front lines in the West, prepares to fire. They have all received a coating of white paint, more than likely whilst still serving in the East. All the 10.5cm (4.1in) leFH 18/2 L/28 howitzers are in the elevated firing position. The *Wespe*'s main gun could traverse up to 17 degrees left or right of the centreline. The howitzer had a maximum range of 4,120 metres (13,500yds). The vehicle had an operational range of 200km (125 miles) by road and 113km (70 miles) over rough terrain. This made the *Wespe* quite an adaptable vehicle, especially in the hills of the Ardennes. During the offensive the vehicle served in the armoured artillery battalions of the *SS* Panzer divisions.

ABOVE: A rare photograph showing soldiers of the 12th *SS Panzer* Division *Hitlerjugend* firing a 7.5cm (3in) gun during the opening phases of the Ardennes offensive in December 1944. The *Hitlerjugend* Division was given the task of taking part in the preliminary bombardment of American positions prior to sending armour and troops through the cold misty morning of 16 December. The Americans forces were taken completely by surprise by the attack and were overrun by superior *Hitlerjugend* and other *Waffen-SS* troops near the village of Rocherath. However, in spite of their initial success in this area the 12th *SS* were soon ground down in a battle of attrition. By 20 December the division had received a severe mauling east of Rocherath and Krinkelt. Around the town of Bastogne significant numbers of *Hitlerjugend* fought to the death attempting to break through into the ravaged town, but their efforts were in vain.

BELOW: *Waffen-SS* grenadiers are compelled to withdraw from the Ardennes by intense American pressure. A whitewashed Pz.Kpfw.IV Ausf H with intact *Schürzen* or 'skirts' provides armoured support. During the early period of the Ardennes offensive the Pz. IV distinguished itself in heavy fighting, and provided a significant proportion of the strengh of *SS* Panzer regiments. In fact, it was this particular Panzer type that spearheaded the force through the Ardennes. *Kampfgruppe* Peiper fielded a mixed force of Pz. IVs and Panthers. Unlike the larger, heavier Panther, the Pz.Kpfw.IV was considered to be better suited to the rugged terrain over which Peiper had to take his spearhead *SS* force. The vehicle also required much less fuel than the Panthers and the monstrous King Tigers, which was a vital consideration.

LEFT: A 15cm (5.9in) *Panzerwerfer* 42 *auf Selbstfahrlafette* Sd.Kfz.4/1 multi-barrelled rocket-launcher is seen somewhere in the Ardennes in early January 1945. The 10-barrel *Nebelwerfer* is mounted on a *Maultier* halftrack – an armoured modification of a standard Opel truck chassis, with tracks replacing the rear wheels. The rockets fired by the Sd.Kfz.4/1 had a range of 6,700m (7,370yds), and they proved lethal against area targets such as troops and convoys of soft-skinned vehicles. The blast effect was so massive that a direct hit could easily confuse an enemy tank crew. The Sd.Kfz.4/1 equipped *Nebelwerfer* brigades on all fronts. The standard *SS* battalion consisted of four batteries of six 15cm rocket launchers, a total of 24 launchers and 144 barrels.

BELOW: A group of *Nashorn* tank destroyers seen early in January 1945. The *Nashorn* mounted a long-barrelled, high-velocity 8.8cm (3.45in) Pak 43/1 L/71 in a lightly armoured rear-fighting compartment constructed on a modified Pz.Kpfw.III/IV tank chassis. The open top of the fighting compartment could be covered in canvas to provide some weather protection. The gun could penetrate over 15cm (5.9in) of sloped armour at a range of 2,000m (2,200yds), which meant that it could destroy most Allied tanks. *Nashorns* were operated by Army tank-hunting *Abteilungen*, but they also provided *SS* Panzer units with long-range fire support. On several occasions on the Eastern Front *Nashorn* crews destroyed Soviet T-34s at ranges of up to 4,500m (4,950yds), and a *Nashorn* accounted for the only U.S. M26 Pershing heavy tank to be destroyed in action.

BELOW: *Hummel* self-propelled guns are loaded on flatbed railway cars for strategic deployment in the West. Like the *Nashorn*, the *Hummel* was based on a modified Pz.III/IV chassis. It mounted a standard 15cm (5.9in) heavy field howitzer, though to save weight ready-use ammunition was limited to 18 rounds.

Although it was not common in the Ardennes, the *SS* did receive the *Hummel* in small quantities. Six were assigned to the single heavy self-propelled artillery battery attached to each Army and *Waffen-SS* Panzer division. Virtually all of them were destroyed as a result of extensive Allied fighter-bomber attacks.

RIGHT: An interesting shot of a *Waffen-SS* StuG III Ausf G assault gun in action against American positions early in January 1945. By this stage of the battle the German armoured spearheads, bedevilled by broken lines of communication and a lack of fuel, had ground to a halt. The Allies were rapidly rearranging forces to create a firm defensive line, and were making plans for their own advance east. *SS* soldiers and armoured crews constantly found themselves beating the enemy at terrible cost, only to find fresh, well-armed American troops waiting for them a few miles on. Hitler ordered that an attempt be made to reinforce Manteuffel's army – then stalled near the town of Celles, just five miles from the Meuse. The 9th *Panzer* and 15th *Panzergrenadier* Divisions were released from reserve, but the attempt failed in the face of a relentless counteroffensive by the US VII Corps,

commanded by General 'Lightning Joe' Collins. This German failure marked the turning point of the offensive: from now on it would be the Allied armies which dictated the pace of operations.

ABOVE: *Waffen-SS* Panzergrenadiers inside a trench during the last stages of the Ardennes offensive. The soldier is using a periscope to allow him to observe the enemy while minimising his exposure to hostile fire. By this stage of the campaign the Germans were firmly on the defensive, or were compelled to withdraw. The huge numbers of Allied reinforcements arriving in the Ardennes meant that even Hitler had to realize just how dangerous the war in the West had become.

On 8 January 1945, he grudgingly ordered a retreat to a line running south from Dochamps, in the Samree-Baraque de Fraiture area, to Longchamps, 8km (5 miles) north of Bastogne. Even more significantly he ordered the mighty *SS Panzer* divisions to go over to the defensive. The Sixth *Panzer* Army was withdrawn into reserve by Hitler's personal command and he also called back the remnants of his favourite fighting machine – the *SS Leibstandarte* – from Bastogne.

DEFENDING THE REICH

Despite her soldiers' best efforts, the Reich no longer had any answer to the superior firepower of the advancing Allied armies.

After the almost inevitable failure of the Ardennes offensive, even the most fanatical of Hitler's followers could no longer avoid the truth. Germany's armed forces had shot their bolt, and the *Wehrmacht* no longer had the strength to stop the Allies. Out on the battlefield, fighting on the borders of the Fatherland, their homeland, troops realized that, barring miracles, the war was lost (though this was seldom admitted openly). Even the fanatics of the *SS* were

LEFT: A group of *Waffen-SS* troops man a 2cm (0.78in) Flak 38 light anti-aircraft gun in action on the western frontiers of the Reich. By January 1945, Hitler's Germany was fighting for its survival. The Reich that was to have lasted a millennium was about to be invaded from both east and west. Although the nation still had some 10 million men (and women and children) under arms, over four million had been killed in action since the beginning of the war. Following the defeat in the Ardennes, Hitler knew that new measures were needed to prevent what he called the 'two-fold devastation of the Reich'.

losing their faith in a German victory. Under-armed and undermanned, the *Wehrmacht*'s infantry and Panzer divisions were burnt-out remnants of their former selves. Driven by necessity, ageing *Volkssturm* and teenaged *Hitlerjugend* units were thrown into line along with veteran soldiers and elite troops of the *SS*.

By late November 1944, British and American forces had punched their way through into Alsace and the German 19th Army had fallen back to improvised and weak defensive positions on the left bank of the Rhine. Just prior to the Ardennes offensive, *SS-Reichsführer* Heinrich Himmler had been appointed Commander-in-Chief of the Upper Rhine. Almost immediately Himmler formed a defensive front, mobilised units from his Replacement Army from the Eastern Front, and reinforced Army Group Upper Rhine.

In early January 1945, a quickly thrown-together force of stragglers, *Volkssturm*, *Hitlerjugend*, customs officials, flak auxiliaries, and battalions of non-Germans from the East, propped-up by a few *SS* units, made an ambitious attack with two divisions within a few miles of Strasbourg. However, by 20 January the Allies counterattacked and rolled up Himmler's bridgehead west of the Rhine. Within four weeks the *Reichsführer's* offensive in the West was over, and the remnants of his forces were being driven back across the Rhine with massive casualties.

In March, the German defences along the Rhine were then broken in two places by the Allies, and multiple Rhine crossings threatened the annihilation of German forces in the West. Fierce fighting continued to rage as the Allies pushed deeper into the interior of a bombed and devastated Reich. While British and Canadian armies pressed on through northern Germany, aiming for Hamburg, the US Ninth and First Armies began a huge encirclement of the Ruhr, which was finally completed by 1 April 1945, forcing the surrender of some 325,000 men of Walter Model's Army Group B.

On other parts of the Western Front, both *Wehrmacht* and *SS* units continued to resist as they fell back. Here, Allied troops fought against groups of fanatical German soldiers determined to maintain their positions, at any cost. That cost was high, especially since the *Wehrmacht*'s ranks were now being bolstered by hastily created ad hoc formations that suffered more casualties than regular units. This was due to the fact that they lacked both experience and capable commanders. Whenever they were thrown into battle, they had to look to neighbouring veteran *Wehrmacht* or *SS* units for assistance or any expertise.

> ‘Small groups of fanatics, the scourge and the terror of the civilian population, fought on to the very end. But little by little, most of the *SS* lost the will to fight.’

This influx of men did not alleviate the deteriorating situation. Neither did the host of new weapons that had entered service at this late stage of the war. Assault guns and tank destroyers were cheaper and quicker to build than tanks, and they were used as Panzer replacements in *Wehrmacht* and *SS* divisions. But although they were suited to defensive war, they could not make a difference. By the beginning of 1945, even the elite *SS* units in the West could not offset the vastly unequal odds. What made matters even worse was that the bulk of the most capable Army and *SS* divisions were tied down on the Eastern Front, some being used in a doomed attempt to retake the Hungarian oilfelds and others spending blood trying to contain the Red Army as it drove unstoppably for the River Oder.

It was these divisions in the East that acquired Germany's latest and most effective equipment. But the *SS* of 1945 was very different from the small, hand-picked, racially pure elite that had been blooded in Poland and France. The *SS* of 1945 was nearly a million strong, and included in that number many non-German volunteer formations that were, by the last months of the war, poorly trained and very inexperienced. Even the cream of the veteran *SS* soldiers, who had fought

ABOVE: In spite of the Allies penetrating parts of the frontiers of the Reich, *SS* units were determined at all costs to fight to the bitter end. Here, a battery of *Hummel* self-propelled howitzers advances through the snow in January 1945. In that month, *SS-Reichsführer* Heinrich Himmler assembled a force of stragglers, *Volkssturm*, *Hitlerjugend*, custom officials, flak auxiliaries, and battalions of non-Germans from the East, supported by a few *SS* units. Himmler had no military experience, and was totally unfit to command a battalion, let alone an entire Army Group. The failure of his forlorn offensive was inevitable, and as the equally inevitable Allied counterattacks punched through thinly-held German positions, the *Reichsführer* declared himself sick with a stomach complaint and retreated to a sanatorium. By March, British and American armies directed at the German heartland were ready to cross the Rhine in force.

with great skill and tenacity through Normandy, the Ardennes, Arnhem and then to the frontiers of the Reich, were shadows of their former selves.

German troops were slowly being squeezed from East and West. On the evening of 11 April, the US Ninth Army reached the River Elbe. At Magdeburg an armoured division seized a bridge-head across the Elbe and the next day an American division established another at Barby.

By the time the American forces had enlarged the bridgehead on 14 April, only 8km (50 miles) separated them from the German lines to Berlin. Defeat now seemed imminent, and the only choice remaining to the last tattered formations of the *Wehrmacht* and *SS* was to fight to the death in the East, to allow as many Germans as possible to flee to the relative safety of the West where they could surrender to the advancing Anglo-Americans.

LEFT: Part of a *Nebeltruppe* brigade laying out shells for their 15cm (5.9in) *Nebelwerfer* 41 rocket launcher. This six-barrelled rocket launcher was mounted on the carriage of the 3.7cm (1.45in) Pak 35/36. The *Nebelwerfer* was an infantry support weapon that provided the direct and indirect support necessary to prevail on the battlefield in defence or attack. Although the *Nebelwerfer* was potentially a lethal weapon, which caused unprecedented damage when accurately fired on target, by January 1945 independent *SS Nebeltruppe* brigades became a rarity in the West as they were more in use against the massive Russian assault in the East.

ABOVE: On a road in February 1945 is an 8.8cm (3.45in) flak gun surrounded by a number of support vehicles. In the western parts of Germany, especially in the big cities, such as Cologne, many inhabitants were now prepared to pay the price of foreign military occupation if it meant the end of the Allied bombing campaign on homes and factories. However, there were still a great many genuine strongholds determined to hold to the party line of resisting at all costs.

Along the river Rhine positions were heavily fortified and reinforced. Troops set up tank traps or sited heavy flak guns on main roads. A number of *SS* soldiers were assigned to special engineer demolition teams tasked with blowing up bridges, while others were used to terrorize villages and small towns, plastering them with threatening signs and slogans, warning the population that they would be executed if they were to try to surrender to the enemy.

RIGHT: An *SS* Panzergrenadier section takes up a defensive position as a local counterattack against the Allies gets under way. The MG42 machine gunners are supporting two late-variant Pz.Kpfw.IVs complete with turret and side skirting. By January–February 1945 Panzers in the rapidly shrinking Reich were better armed than ever before, but lacked adequately trained crews. With all reserves gone, the *Panzerwaffe* was only a shadow of its former self. It had already exhausted virtually all its ammunition and fuel supplies. More and more armoured vehicles were sent back into the line as loosely organized ad hoc groups, thrown together in a mixed and disorganized manner.

ABOVE: A unit of StuG III assault guns prepare for action in the West in January 1945. Vehicles rarely formed up in the open like this, since to do so was to invite attack from the Allied fighter-bombers which ranged at will in the skies over the Reich. Allied air superiority made any movement by day a serious risk. Air attack was not the only danger, however. By this time, Germany's industry and transport infrastructure was in ruins, and fuel was in extremely short supply.

The fuel famine meant that many vehicles were simply abandoned after running out of petrol. Although the end was certain, most German armoured units continued to fight until the last days. However, there was a difference between the Eastern and Western Fronts: in the West, units out of fuel and ammunition were likely to surrender. In the East, by contrast, units were likely to fight on as infantry, before trying to escape westwards to surrender to the Americans or British.

ABOVE: An unusual photograph showing an *SS* motor-cyclist wearing an issue fur cap and a non-standard greatcoat lined with fur. The gasmask is not being worn due to the threat of a gas attack, but more than likely to protect his face from the cold January temperatures along the Rhine in 1945. Late in 1944, propaganda posters were still appealing to the German nation to hand over unwanted winter clothing to their 'brave soldiers at the front'. However, in the chaotic state of late-war Germany, military winter clothing was no longer being produced or distributed. It was therefore left to the individual soldiers either to use items of civilian clothing or to 'acquire' warm gear from the bodies of the dead.

ABOVE: Hastily recruited *SS* troops train with the 7.5cm (2.95in) Pak 40 heavy anti-tank gun. Early in 1945, small Pak units were formed from training schools and the young men were immediately sent into combat, often paying a high price for their inexperience. A number of these improvised anti-tank units were stationed along the Rhine in a futile attempt to prevent the Allies from crossing. However, within weeks of their deployment the remnants of Himmler's motley collection of exhausted recruits and old men were being driven back across the Rhine with massive casualties. Soon the Allies were across the Rhine in two places, with the British driving for Hamburg and the Americans threatening the Ruhr.

LEFT: The crew of a 2cm (0.78in) Flak 38 anti-aircraft gun overlooks a road just north of Hamburg. It was in wooded areas in this region that small groups of die-hard *SS* detachments and special guerrilla teams called *Werewolves* roamed the countryside, sniping and sabotaging Allied vehicles. They set up decapitation wires across roads, laid mines and threatened the local population with execution if they provided the British with information. Special leaflets were prepared giving detailed instructions of 'National defence procedures'. 'Take anything from the enemy you can,' they read. 'His front lines depend on what rear areas can send him. So the more you take away from him, the more you will be doing for your country.' What the German government was appealing for was mass Nazi partisan warfare. In Berlin's eyes, the *SS* was to play a significant part in this 'struggle for survival'.

ABOVE: A soldier shows conscripts how to use the deadly *Panzerfaust*. This simple weapon not only gave the *SS* grenadiers a viable anti-tank capability, but its ease of use allowed *Volkssturm*, *Hitlerjugend* and even civilians to be armed with them. A number of *SS* troops were detailed to familiarize the *Volkssturm* and *Hitlerjugend* recruits with the *Panzerfaust*, Mauser rifles, machine guns and hand grenades. All men between the ages of 16 and 60 capable of bearing arms in defence of the Fatherland were ordered to recruiting stations all across Germany to join the *Volkssturm*. Their numbers included those previously classed as medically unfit to fight in the front lines. Although better trained than the British Home Guard of four years before, the German home defence units were still at a distinct disadvantage when they were thrown into battle against the veteran Allied armies attacking from East and West.

LEFT: A *Wehrmacht* officer confers with an *SS* Panzergrenadier from his Sd.Kfz.251 halftrack. With the defences along the Rhine now broken, Allied forces pushed on deeper into Germany. The objective for the Americans was the industrial area of the Ruhr, and the pincer arms of First and Ninth Armies closed at Lippstadt on 1 April 1945. Through that massive encirclement the industrial heart of the Ruhr was prised open, and the whole body of German Army Group B was trapped. The Army Group Commander, Field Marshal Model, shot himself rather than capitulate to the enemy. Over 325,000 men and a further 100,000 soldiers of the Flak batteries which had guarded the Ruhr marched into captivity.

ABOVE: With a convoy of halftracks in the background, a motley group including both *Wehrmacht* and *SS* troops take a break somewhere in Western Germany early in March 1945. They are using a roadside ditch to provide minimal protection from Allied air attack. A number of the soldiers are wearing the general-issue padded, hooded, reversible jacket in an autumn burred- edge pattern. The rest of the men are in pullover parkas and overtrousers for winter wear. This padded grey/white suit was common to both *Wehrmacht* and *SS* troops and was the first truly reversible cold-weather uniform that offered the wearer both concealment and extra warmth. By this period of the war, with military clothing stocks at a premium, a non-existent quartermaster organisation and no reliable means of transportation, most of these soldiers are wearing a mixture of *Wehrmacht* and *SS* winter wear.

RIGHT: The Allied bombing campaign against Germany continued into the last months of the war, and the *Luftwaffe*'s anti-aircraft batteries continued to take a toll from the US Eighth Air Force and Bomber Command of the Royal Air Force. The 8.8cm (3.45in) Flak 41 gun was the most common heavy AA weapon, and is seen here being fired in March 1945. This heavy calibre gun was capable of engaging aircraft flying as high as 10,600m (34,788ft). The 'Acht-Acht' was specifically designed as a dual purpose weapon, and had proved itself as a highly effective tank-killer from before the invasion of Poland. It was originally manned by the *Luftwaffe*, but flak crews were eventually drawn from the Army, the *SS*, the *Hitlerjugend* and even from female auxiliary organisations. All found the Flak 8.8cm gun a very versatile weapon, and it was used extensively on the Western Front until the end of the war. The gun's high mount could make it easy to spot, but properly sited with a good field of fire, the gun was a major threat to advancing enemy armour and artillery.

ABOVE: An *SS* Tiger tank moving through a burning village. This was one of a handful of Tigers left on the Western Front. While many Germans were now ready to surrender, Allied troops were as likely to encounter fanatical units that unflinchingly maintained their positions, despite the cost and regardless of their life. Ultimately Allied tanks exploited these fanatical German defensive positions, moving across country in sweeping advances and outflanking attacks. In effect,

the Allies conducted a *Blitzkrieg* campaign in reverse. By isolating hold-out units like this, the Allies were able to consolidate their hold on the rest of the country, crushing all remaining resistance until the Germans were compelled to surrender. Although individual German units still possessed the ability to maul the Allies in small local battles, temporarily impeding any advance, they lacked sufficient power to change the situation decisively.

RIGHT: Many *SS* soldiers still clung to the ardent belief that they were superhuman beings on the battlefield, in spite of the evidence to the contrary presented by the overwhelming Allied superiority in manpower and firepower. They continued to fight on. Here, an independent battery of *SS* rocket launchers fires on an attacking Allied force. *Nebelwerfers* could be deadly to an unprotected enemy position. Following the saturation of the area with high-explosives, normally supported by what remaining armour they could muster, the *SS* attempted to bulldoze their way through the hail of Allied anti-tank fire, using what cover they could find. However, with little or no military organisation or communication available, even the *SS* could not gather enough force to launch a truly effective strike against its enemies.

ABOVE: With every kind of vehicle in short supply, *SS* troops were compelled to use whatever transport they could get to move heavy equipment. Here, a field car has been pressed into service to tow an old 3.7cm (1.45in) Pak 35/36 anti-tank gun. These troops are withdrawing along a road somewhere in southern Germany in February 1945. All the soldiers are wearing white snow camouflage clothing, and many can be seen with the M43 *Einheitsfeldmütze*. This field cap became the standard headdress worn by the *SS* from September 1943. It is likely that this is an ad hoc unit formed from any troops available in the area. Because the men in such units did not know each other and had different levels of training, they were less effective than homogeneous units, and often suffered heavier casualties than regular *SS* formations.

RIGHT: A group of *Wehrmacht* and *SS* Panzer officers still manage to share a joke despite the dire military situation in the West. Two of the officers are wearing the green splinter-pattern *Wehrmacht* camouflage used on the heavy reversible winter uniforms, whilst the other men are wearing the mouse-grey camouflage versions. No form of insignia decoration or badge other than special rank insignia for this type of winter camouflage clothing was worn on this uniform. The Panzer officer in the centre is holder of the Knight's Cross, with Oakleaves and Swords.

BELOW: A lone Tiger tank supports an *SS* unit making a counterattack late in January 1945. Note the smoke dischargers and extra track links attached to the turret. In many areas the Allies found the quality of their opposition very uneven. At one moment a handful of them were receiving wholesale enemy surrenders; at the next, an entire division was being held up by the stubborn resistance of just one single *SS* unit and an armoured vehicle. Possibly the biggest threat came from ambushes or even individual snipers. Operating from concealed positions and with an absolute minimum use of force, they could hold up an Allied advance. Such stealthy attacks were detested by the Allies as much for the nervousness that they caused to men's routine movements in forward areas as for the casualties that they inflicted.

ABOVE: An *SS* grenadier preparing to use his deadly *Panzerschreck* or 'Tank Terror' weapon against advancing Allied armour. The *Panzerschreck* was inspired by the American Bazooka, though being of larger calibre had a much greater effect. The weapon consisted of a metal tube that fired a rocket-propelled hollow-charge anti-tank shell that weighed 3.3kg (7.2lb). Unlike the *Panzerfaust* anti-tank weapon, the *Panzerschreck* was reusable and not discarded after firing. The weapon was more accurate than the *Panzerfaust* and during the last year of the war it scored a number of successes against the ever-increasing forces of Allied tanks driving into Germany.

However, the limited range of the weapon meant that its operator had to get in close to guarantee a kill, which required great courage, skill and tenacity. Note the rounded shield mounted in front of the trigger mechanism. This was intended to protect the operator from the rocket's powerful back-blast – earlier models did not have this feature, and any man firing the weapon risked severe scorching. Unfortunately, the blast of the rocket propellant hitting the shield gave the *Panzerschreck* – actual designation the RPzB.54 or *Raketenpanzerbüchse* 54 – a nasty kickback. Effective range varied from 100m (110yds) for moving targets to more than 700m (770yds) for fixed targets.

ABOVE: *SS* and *Wehrmacht* Panzergrenadiers withdraw as the Allies smash another defensive position in the West. Everywhere the Allies probed the defences looking for weak spots. They infiltrated everywhere, using their mobility to cut off large numbers of defenders. In most cases German troops, even the fanatical SS, were forced to withdraw by the overwhelming Allied strength. A few true believers in the *Führer*, often young idealists who had been brought up through the ranks of the *Hitlerjugend*, objected violently to being ordered to withdraw, preferring to fight to the bitter end.

LEFT: Fixed German defences varied considerably in strength. Some of the weapons were mounted in strong concrete emplacements, covering all likely approaches through minefields and ditches surrounding strategically important areas. Others, like this armoured half-track mounting a 2cm (0.78in) *Flakvierling* 38 quadruple anti-aircraft gun, were simply dug in to a defensive position. By this stage of the war, flak guns were used extensively and effectively in ground combat on the defensive lines that the Germans established on the Western Front. Most such positions included dugout sleeping quarters for the crew and storage for food and ammunition.

LEFT: In a forest somewhere on the Western Front an *SS* soldier takes aim with a *Sturmgewehr* 44 – the world's first true assault rifle – combining the characteristics of an ordinary rifle and a sub-machine gun. Firing a lower-powered round, the StG44 was as accurate as a rifle at all practical combat ranges, but was also capable of controllable fully automatic fire. Small numbers were used successfully on trials, and full production was authorised in July 1944. More than 425,000 examples were produced in the last months of the war, at a unit cost of only 66 Reichsmarks. Soldiers carried six 30-round magazines; together with the magazine attached to the weapon, the default ammo load out for a fully equipped soldier was seven magazines, totalling 210 rounds.

ABOVE: An *SS* Flak crew moves an 8.8cm (3.45in) Flak gun into position following futile and costly defensive fighting against British attacks. By this period of the war *SS* commanders still struggled desperately to hold their forces together. They were paralysed by developments they had not expected and could not organize their formations in the utter confusion that now ensued on the battlefield. In many areas the collapse of communication systems had left individual units isolated, unable to establish contact with higher command or with neighbouring units. As a result, tactical decisions were almost invariably taken late, and were often disastrously overtaken by events, with one position after another being lost to the Allies.

ABOVE: An 8.8cm (3.45in) Flak gun is used in ground combat during a stubborn defensive action in January 1945. Ultimate catastrophe now threatened the German forces. Again and again SS units fought superbly and with great bravery, but proved unable to generate the weight of fighting power necessary to slow the Allied advance. They now lacked the capacity to carry out an objective or withstand a counter-attack. The position in the West was not made any easier by the withdrawal of Sepp Dietrich's Sixth SS Panzer Army, transferred to Hungary on the direct orders of the Führer, where it was ordered to relieve Budapest and retake the Hungarian oilfields. Meanwhile the troops it left behind were forced to retreat, taking casualties under the continuous pounding by Allied tactical aircraft and long-range artillery.

ABOVE: One of the many hundreds of 8.8cm (3.45in) Flak gun defensive positions erected by the *Luftwaffe*, the *Wehrmacht* and the *SS* during the last defence of the Reich in 1945. The *SS* was now a long way from the aggressive, fast-moving force of 1940. Battles were not settled by movement, on the German side at least. To the defenders of the Reich the war had settled down to a losing battle of attrition, with the overwhelming might of the Allies wearing them down blow by blow. To an *SS* man in 1945, victories were achieved by disrupting and delaying the enemy. Although it was not something they openly expressed, most *SS* men had become aware of their own weakness in the dying months of the war. Commanders almost always displayed a fear of being over-run. They had no ability to attack in the old *SS* tradition: instead, Hitler's bodyguard had become a force which more often, when threatened, struck out on all sides in an attempt to ward off destruction, or possibly simply to find a way of escape.

BELOW: An *SS Marder* self-propelled gun in action in early 1945. It has a coat of white winter camouflage paint over its dark sand base but there is no evidence of the divisional emblem normally painted on the side of the fighting compartment. Although a rarity by this period of the war, both *SS* and *Wehrmacht* tanks and self-propelled guns were still occasionally seen leading attacks across the battlefield in small numbers. As they approached enemy emplacements, they allowed the infantry to sweep past to deal with anti-tank guns, before the armour once again took over. The Allies were frequently shocked by the speed at which an entire unit could be transformed into a ruin by an apparently outnumbered and defeated enemy. *SS* Panzergrenadiers in particular, driven by their National Socialist indoctrination and by blind faith in the *Führer*, constantly exhibited an aggressive spirit and caused the Allies many casualties.

FINAL DEFEAT

As March drew into April 1945, the Allies were approaching Berlin from both East and West. It was clear that the Americans would be more kindly victors than the Russians.

But it soon became apparent to German units defending lines to the west of Berlin that Allied forces were no longer making any serious attempts at smashing their way through to the Reich capital. It was therefore feared that the capture of Berlin was to be exclusively left to the Red Army. By this period of the war even most *Waffen-SS* soldiers fighting in mixed units in the West realised that the war was irrevocably lost. Few of them harboured any illusions at the kind of treatment they would receive as prisoners of the Russians. The majority of *Waffen-SS* men did not expect to survive Soviet captivity, and it was therefore imperative that when the time came to surrender they would rather lay down their arms to the Anglo-Americans than to the Soviets. It was this underlying fear of being captured by Red Army forces that prompted a

LEFT: Defending to the last, an *SS* flamethrower destroys a village as the Germans retreat before the advancing Allies. Overwhelmed by increasing losses, commanders in the field were becoming increasingly defeatist. Their armies had been broken up, and their armour almost expended. They were battle weary, knowing that even fully armed and equipped they could never handle Allied air superiority.

number of both *Wehrmacht* and *Waffen-SS* units to capitulate to the West, rather than undertake a staunch fighting withdrawal to the East, and be annihilated by forward echelons of the advancing Soviet Army. In a number of areas many *SS* soldiers were already stripping their uniforms of identifying insignia to avoid persecution if they fell into enemy hands.

Although most of the *SS* men may have known that the end of the war was near, many still retained intense unit pride, which ensured they would do their duty to the bitter end. The realisation of defeat also inspired the fanatical units that were to ardently follow Hitler's infamous 'scorched earth' policy. Special 'Demolition Troops' were trained by *SS* soldiers and deployed to help in the destruction of factories, mines, and bridges. Some were expected to get involved in guerrilla activity, and planned to mine buildings likely to be used as billets or headquarters by Anglo–American forces. The *SS* also became involved in supporting special units primarily raised not for home defence duties, but to 'mobilize a spirit of national resistance' among the weary population. This band of men fanned out across their own assigned areas and searched out and lynched civilians that were regarded by the Party as 'collaborators and defeatists'.

Another planned guerrilla movement was created by *Reichsführer-SS* Heinrich Himmler and trained exclusively by the *SS*. The *Werewolf* volunteers were to be deployed as assassination squads and demolition teams alongside special *SS* sabotage units. Himmler was aware that these guerrilla operations in Germany would not win the war; their task was to use terror to delay the advancing enemy long enough to allow for a political settlement favourable to a crumbling Reich. In the event, the final collapse of the Reich was so complete and so fast that few of these murderous plans were ever put into effect.

By April 1945 the *SS* divisions no longer existed except in name. What remained were shadows, their ranks partially filled with a motley collection of men from the *Wehrmacht*, *Kriegsmarine* and *Luftwaffe*. Old veterans of World War I were also drafted into battle to bolster the dwindling ranks.

But unlike their *SS* counterparts, they were not fighting with fanaticism in the name of the *Führer*; they were out there on the battlefield for the survival of themselves and their families.

Despite the impossible situation facing Germany during the last weeks of the war, there were a number of well-seasoned *SS* commanders that tried to hold what remained of their men together with remarkable discipline. Inside what was known as Fortress Berlin, *SS* troops from the Western Front helped make up the numbers of

---

The last and most fanatical defenders of Berlin were a *kampfgruppe* from the *SS-Leibstandarte* commanded by Wilhelm Mohnke.

---

troops defending the sprawling city to some 200,000. But that was a pittance, when compared to the million or more Red Army men advancing against the city from the East.

Because supplies were so desperately low soldiers were given a wide range of arms. There were at least 15 different types of rifles and 10 kinds of machine guns in use during the final defence of Berlin, many of which had been salvaged from a number of occupied countries.

Outside Berlin, Anglo-American forces were clearing the way to victory in the West. The British and Canadians fought the last remaining pockets of resistance in the north, whilst in the South American and French armies overran Bavaria and pushed through into Austria and carried on to within 50 km (30 miles) of both Prague and Vienna. It was in Austria in the town of Steyr that the 9th *SS-Panzer* Division *Hohenstaufen* surrendered to the Americans, alongside what remained of the *Leibstandarte Adolf Hitler*, following its desperate and costly retreat from the clutches of the Red Army. The remnants of the most fanatical of all *SS* divisions, the 12th *SS-Panzer* Division *Hitlerjugend*, also managed to escape from the advancing Russian forces and surrendered to the

LEFT: March 1945, and *SS* Panzergrenadiers are hitching a lift on board a self-propelled 2cm (0.78in) anti-aircraft gun. The halftrack is towing ammunition for the flak gun. By this time, the remnants of the *Waffen-SS* on the Western Front no longer expected total victory. Nevertheless, virtually all *SS* soldiers still felt an absolute sense of loyalty to unit and *Führer*. Younger men had never known any other leader than Hitler, and some were sustained by a mixture of fatalism and blind faith that the man they had been taught to worship would work a last miracle.

American army near Enns. The 16th *SS-Panzer-grenadier* Division *Reichsführer-SS* handed itself over to the British and American forces at Radstadt and Klagenfurt. The 17th *SS-Panzer-grenadier* Division *Götz von Berlichingen* finally surrendered to American troops near Achensee on 7 May.

These battle-weary survivors had fought with undoubted courage against massively superior enemy numbers in the East and the West, but at a fearsome cost. The *Hitlerjugend* Division went to war in Normandy in June 1944 with a fighting strength of 21,300 teenaged *SS* men. Only 455 exhausted troops – notwithstanding the reinforcements sent to the division – survived the next 10 months to surrender to the U.S. Army.

In spite of its ultimate defeat, the *Waffen-SS* was without doubt a unique military formation. Although its methods and aggressiveness have often been called into question, the enemies who fought against its members, especially against the premier *SS* divisions, have never doubted its effectiveness and fighting skill on the battlefield. As fighting soldiers they were an elite band of men who were arrogant, and at the same time courageous and effective.

The failure of German troops to change the outcome of events in the West in 1944 was not due to lack of skill or tenacity. Germany was simply stretched too far, fighting three of the world's great military powers on three fronts. The *SS* did make some difference: its performance in Normandy, at Arnhem and in the Ardennes prevented Anglo-American forces from reaching Germany a lot sooner than they did. But in the fierce battles in the East and West the original elite *Waffen-SS* was all but destroyed. All that was left was used up in a desperate and ultimately futile effort designed to help prop up the collapsing German armies on the Eastern Front.

ABOVE: An Sd.Kfz.251 halftrack and two supply trucks withdraw across a small river in March 1945. All along the Allied fronts a succession of large- and small-scale actions took place, driving vital wedges into the ever-weakening German defences. German strongpoints were being knocked out by Allied infantry, armour, artillery and air power. Nevertheless, in spite of the overwhelming might of the Allied

armies, *SS* grenadiers fought extraordinarily well, given their isolation, the lack of manpower and the paucity of their supplies and equipment. The Germans were great opportunists on the battlefield, regardless of how bad the situation seemed to be. They were always prepared to act, and could never quite understand why their more careful Allied opponents sometimes seemed reluctant to exploit their successes fully.

RIGHT: A 7.5cm (2.95in) Pak 40 anti-tank gun in early January 1945. The crew have attempted to break up the gun's shape by using white sheeting wrapped around the barrel and gun wheel. Although it is difficult to identify in this photograph, note how well the German troops have camouflaged a prime mover with an 8.8cm (3.45in) Flak gun on tow parked against a farm building in the distance. All German soldiers feared Allied fighter bombers: even veteran soldiers entered the battlefield feeling helpless against the paralysing effect of air bombardment. As with all German troops, what was left of the *SS* units was therefore compelled to move chiefly by night to avoid detection by the Allied pilots roaming at will over the Reich.

ABOVE: An *SS* mortar crew making final adjustments to the weapon's mount prior to it being used in anger. None of the *SS* divisions stationed in the West prior to the Allied invasion of Normandy in June 1944 had received mortars. Following the invasion of northern France, *SS* units were authorised two heavy motorised companies, each equipped with a dozen 12cm (4.7in) mortars. The *SS* soon found that mortars were an excellent defensive weapon and provided machine-gun nests and other defensive positions with additional firepower in order to sustain themselves successfully on the battlefield.

LEFT: Seen hiding in undergrowth during the desperate defensive battles on the Western Front are two well-concealed *SS* men, both armed with the lethal *Panzerschreck*. During the last frantic months of the war the *SS* and their *Wehrmacht* counterparts came to increasingly rely on man-portable weapons in order to provide anti-tank defence against Allied armour. Each *SS* Tank Destruction company was well equipped with *Panzerfausts*, *Panzerschrecks*, anti-tank mines and light infantry weapons. During the last days of the war the *Waffen-SS* employed a variety of demolition charges against tanks. Some of them were magnetised to allow them to stick to the sides of tanks.

ABOVE: Early 1945 and a *Waffen-SS* crew prepares to fire a 10.5cm (4.13in) leFH 18M. Originally an infantry support weapon, it was pressed into service in an anti-tank role in Russia when it was found to be one of the few German guns capable of dealing with Soviet T-34s and KV-1s. For most of the war, each German infantry, Panzer, and motorized division was allocated at least two full battalions of three four-gun batteries of leFH 18 howitzers for their divisional artillery regiments. By 1945, surviving leFH 18s were issued with armour-piercing and shaped-charge shells for engaging tanks directly, as well as with standard high-explosive shells for indirect fire against troops – that is, when they received any ammunition at all.

RIGHT: The driver of an Sd.Kfz.2 *kleines Kettenkraftrad*, or *Kettenrad* for short, transports two *SS* soldiers through a stream somewhere on the Western Front in March 1945. Based on a motorcycle, the Sd.Kfz.2 was the smallest halftrack in regular use. Inevitably, despite the constant Allied bombing, despite the spectre of the British and American forces spearheading towards the very boundaries of Berlin itself, despite the shrinking of the German Army as the enemy pressed in from the west, there were those *SS* soldiers who accepted the hardships they were undergoing as a kind of purgatory – as a tempering and refining of their devotion to their beloved *Führer* and his aims. Once they had demonstrated their loyalty, everything would surely be all right. A dwindling number of fanatics were still convinced that not only would Berlin never fall, but also that victory for Germany would be secured by their ardent National Socialist belief, and by the *Führer*'s genius.

LEFT: *SS* Flak crew guarding one of the many roads leading east towards Berlin. By the first two weeks of April 1945 it became apparent that the capture of the Reich capital was to be exclusively left to the Red Army. Even for the elite remnants of the once mighty *SS*, the battle had become very hard going, and now the possibility of surviving it seemed even more remote. As the defence of the Homeland progressed into its final weeks, the casualty lists rose to massive proportions, making it harder even for *SS* commanders to persuade their men to hold out to the last. In many cases the *SS* determination and will for sacrifice was expended in minor operations for limited objectives too late in the war. The consequences were obvious, and some now lost the will to fight.

LEFT: A group of German soldiers move into action. Although these hard-pressed *SS* troops could no longer affect the situation decisively, they still fought courageously, demonstrating the extent to which a poorly-armed and undermanned force could still resist numerically superior opponents. In an attempt to contain the Allies, there had been spectacular acts of individual heroism and fanaticism, many of which cost the men their lives. What the *SS* hoped to achieve, even though heavily outnumbered, was to keep its enemy everywhere feeling insecure and off balance, while concentrating sufficient forces to dominate decisive points. Unfortunately for the *SS*, the Allies were too strong for it to succeed in its aim.

ABOVE: One of the many anti-tank guns used to defend local areas against enemy armour on the Western Front, in this case a captured Soviet 76.2mm (3in) gun. So many examples of this excellent weapon were taken in 1942 and 1943 that the Germans pressed them into service, and even started manufacturing ammunition for them. As with most Soviet artillery pieces, they were lighter and more effective than their German equivalents, and could fire high-velocity projectiles which made them suitable for use as anti-tank guns as well as divisional or light artillery pieces. Unfortunately for the Germans, the multiplicity of such captured weapons in many different calibres was a quartermaster's nightmare, and by this late stage in the war it was almost impossible to provide the ammunition to keep them in action.

ABOVE: A Flak crew in action in March 1945. The 8.8cm (3.45in) Flak gun has not received any winter camouflage paint and still displays its old summer scheme of brown and green lines over the dark sand base. The gun has just been fired and smoke from its barrel can be seen drifting over the position. In spite of strong Flak defences that covered hundreds of miles of the Western Front, the wholesale collapse in morale resulted in mass surrenders of units swamped by the Allied spearheads. Divisions had disintegrated, leaving scattered bands of demoralized stragglers roaming the countryside without equipment or leadership. By April 1945 what was left of *Wehrmacht*, *Luftwaffe* and *Waffen-SS* formations were shattered ruins of their old selves, with a fraction of their nominal strength and with little or no available armour or artillery support.

ABOVE: *Wehrmacht* and *Waffen-SS* officers inspect a group of female medical auxiliaries. By 1945, German battlefield medical facilities were stretched to the limit and beyond. Medical staff were unable to perform their duties properly, primarily due to severe shortages of medical supplies and transport. As a result, thousands of soldiers on the front lines who would have survived earlier in the war went untreated and died on the battlefield. The Nazis felt that women had no place in uniform, and Germany was slow to enlist female personnel. The armed forces never employed them in the numbers used by the Allies, though by the end of the war many women were serving as *Helferinnen* or 'Helpers' in medical, communications and Flak units.

LEFT: A 2cm (0.78in) Flak gun in action on the Western Front early in 1945. Some *SS* units still tried to use elegance in their tactical manoeuvres, but lacked the control and levels of force to achieve any success. Attrition had done away with many of the most experienced fighters, and their replacements were often of little combat value. Even so, the *SS* still used tightly concentrated infantry and artillery to fight enemy breakthroughs. Hard-won lessons learned in five years of war meant that it could still conceal its movements skilfully, and its fire discipline could still set Allied units back on their heels. However, fighting against such overwhelming odds meant that the *SS* was always doomed to fail.

ABOVE: A 2cm (0.78in) Flak gun crew stands ready for action, looking for American or British tactical fighters. By 1945 Allied air power had all but wiped the *Luftwaffe* from the skies over Germany. What few aircraft were left, including the revolutionary Messerschmitt Me 262 jet, operated out of camouflaged airfields surrounded by large numbers of anti-aircraft weapons. The light flak was particularly deadly, and presented by far the biggest danger to Allied fighter-bombers operating at tree-top level. There were plenty of guns and crews to man them: the Allied bomber offensive had forced Germany to divert nearly two million soldiers and workers and three quarters of its best artillery to defend the Reich.

RIGHT: StuG III Ausf.G assault guns advance towards the rapidly shrinking borders of the Reich. Astonishingly, the *Panzerwaffe* still had some 738 assault guns on strength at the end of the war. Ever since the Allies had landed on the Normandy coast, assault guns had formed an increasing proportion of *SS* armoured strength. Though it was designed as an offensive weapon, the vehicle's low, powerful silhouette and fuel economy made it an excellent defensive weapon. It was successfully used on all fronts, being particularly effective as an anti-armour weapon. The *Sturmgewehr* earned considerable respect both from the crews who used it and from the enemies who encountered it on the battlefield.

ABOVE: Probably the very last Tiger tanks serving on the Western Front in 1945. Although very slow, very heavy and uneconomical to run, the Tiger had earned its deadly reputation in combat on all fronts. Heavily armoured and with a powerful gun, a single Tiger in the right position could dominate the battlefield. However, by the last months of the war, ammunition and fuel supplies were drying up, compelling Tiger crews reluctantly to abandon their tanks, destroying them if

there was time. The Tiger tank was without doubt the most potent armoured killing machine of its era, and its 8.8cm (3.45in) gun could penetrate the armour of American Shermans and British Cromwells at ranges of more than 1,000m (1,100yds). By contrast, most Allied tanks had to get to within point blank range to have a chance of destroying the Tiger. The original version of the tank was succeeded by the even more powerful King Tiger, used in the last battles of the war.

LEFT: An *SS* soldier observes what appears to be a well-concealed 7.5cm (2.95in) leIG 18 light howitzer. The gun has been covered with metal sheeting and *Zeltbahn*. Designed to provide infantry units with close-range fire support, the leIG 18 first entered service in 1929. It weighed only 400kg (882lb) and fired a 6kg (13.2lb) shell to a maximum range of 3,375m (3,692yds). It was the standard light infantry gun at the outbreak of war, and was used by *SS* grenadiers. Infantry guns provided *Waffen-SS* units down to battalion or even company size with their own offensive and defensive fire support without the need to call in artillery support.

LEFT: An *SS* anti-tank gun in action against advancing Allied armour. The large plumes of smoke in the distance suggest that there has been some heavy contact with the enemy. In April 1945 German resistance varied considerably. In many areas the defenders capitulated without firing a shot; in others determined troops fought bitter and prolonged battles until eventually they too surrendered. Both American and British forces were taking whole companies of enemy troops into captivity, complete with NCOs and officers. The situation for the Germans was rapidly deteriorating. Nothing they could do in the field was going to make any difference to the inevitable outcome.

ABOVE: Standing next to his 3.7cm (1.45in) Flak 36 dual-purpose anti-aircraft/anti-armour weapon a gunner scans the horizon for approaching enemy troops. The white bands painted on the splinter shield are kill markings. This crew claims to have scored a remarkable total of 45 kills. Most would have been aircraft, although the Flak 36 was also capable of destroying light armour and softskin vehicles. By April 1945 the Western Allies had reached the Elbe. Although *SS* soldiers still continued to fight them, most available German resources were being thrown at the Red Army's advance in the East.

ABOVE: *SS* Tank Destruction troops advance armed with anti-tank mines. The mine was the most cost-effective German anti-tank weapon of the war. It rarely destroyed enemy tanks completely, but could be relied on to disable them by damaging a track or wheel. *Waffen-SS* grenadiers employed a variety of demolition charges against tanks, pressing into close and dangerous contact with the enemy to score large numbers of kills. By 1945 anti-tank war had become a savage struggle for survival. During the last weeks of the war Army, *SS*, *Hitlerjugend* and *Volkssturm* members necessarily became masters of individual anti-tank tactics, risking (and in many cases losing) their lives in no-quarter close-range combat.

ABOVE: As Germany's collapse begins under repeated Allied hammer blows, two weary *SS* grenadiers festooned with anti-tank weaponry move along a road. In April 1945, American and Soviet units made contact at Torgau, and the Third Reich was cut in half. German forces in the last weeks of the war were to endure one of the greatest nightmares in all of military history.

Roads were clogged by miles of refugees and hordes of defeated soldiers. Those units which still had the will to fight were strung out across a burned and blasted landscape. Men, horse-drawn carts and the few surviving tanks and vehicles struggled eastwards, hoping to buy enough time against the advancing Red Army to allow the refugees to escape to the West.

RIGHT: It took a very brave man to attack a tank armed only with a sticky or magnetic explosive charge. But German troops were used to working with their own tanks, and they knew that the vision from within was so limited that once you got within a few yards of the vehicle the crew could not see you. The biggest danger was getting caught by the tank's tracks.

BELOW: When fuel is at a premium, low-technology means of transport come into their own. The German armed forces were always less highly mechanized than their reputation might have suggested: the triumphs of *Blitzkrieg* in 1939 and 1940 were won by a small mechanized spearhead racing ahead of a horde of marching infantry, supported by horse-drawn logistics. Bicycles are surprisingly effective for moving troops over short distances – and by the spring of 1945 all German combat was over short distances.

ABOVE: War-weary troops withdraw through the ruins of a German town in March 1945. Here a mixed group of exhausted *Waffen-SS* and *Wehrmacht* men trudge along a street following a Pz.Kpfw.IV Ausf.H. During the daylight hours, straggling clusters and columns of German soldiers moved painfully eastward, edging only a few hundred yards at a time, then halting in silence to listen for enemy aircraft. If all was clear, they moved slowly forwards again. When there was time to rest, after hours of desperate tension, the men sank wearily into oblivion by the roadside. They sat in endless filthy, bloody, tired lines, looking for survivors of their own units and collecting them to continue the retreat. Every now and then an officer would take charge, forming an ad hoc *Kampfgruppe* to mount an attack on the enemy.

RIGHT: A group of Demolition Troops move through a forest on the Western Front. One soldier carries a single-shot *Panzerfaust* anti-tank rocket over his shoulder; in front of him another carries a box of ammunition. All over Germany *SS*, *Wehrmacht* and *Volkssturm* Demolition Troops were trained and deployed to enact Hitler's infamous scorched earth policy. Fortunately for the civilians who survived the war, Hitler's intent that the Third Reich should not survive his own demise was short-circuited by Albert Speer and the high command of the *Wehrmacht*, who saw that the *Führer's* orders to start the destruction were never transmitted. It did not stop some *SS* troops from searching out and lynching civilians accused by the Party of being 'collaborators and defeatists'.

ABOVE: A group of Pz.Kpfw.IVs and an Sd.Kfz.251 halftrack advance across a field in broad daylight. The good condition of the uncamouflaged vehicles probably indicates that the photo was taken in the autumn of 1944. By the end of the war in May 1945 the combined strength of the *Panzerwaffe* was 2,023 tanks, 738 assault guns and 159 Flak Panzers. Unbelievably, this was almost the same strength with which the *Wehrmacht* had attacked Russia in June 1941. Although the Panzer divisions still existed on paper, they lacked organization and command structures. Many of their tank crews were inexperienced, for most of the old veterans and many of the unit commanders had been killed in action.

LEFT: The last defence in the West. An *SS* gun crew opens fire during a futile and costly battle against advancing enemy armour. Note the number of expended shell cases on the ground. During the last few months of the war there was a large influx of soldiers drafted into the *Waffen-SS* and *Wehrmacht* with little or no training. Morale and combat effectiveness suffered. Few of these new recruits believed in the *Führer* or victory, but they continued to resist the invading Allies to a surprising extent. Because they were fighting for their homes and families, they made up for their inexperience with equal parts of desperation and courage.

RIGHT: An interesting photograph showing *Waffen-SS*, *Wehrmacht* and *Fallschirmjäger* troops discussing the military situation in front of a StuG III Ausf.G. At the end of the war it was not unusual to see such a mixed group of soldiers fighting together, especially after pockets of German resistance had been isolated by the advancing Allies. Anyone who could hold and fire a weapon was swept up into temporary battlegroups, attempting to break out to safer areas. But it would not be long before there were no safe areas left.

ABOVE: The *Waffen-SS* started World War II as the Nazi Party's private army, a bodyguard force for Adolf Hitler. Small in number, it was an elite fighting force whose aggression and training were decisive on many battlefields. As World War II progressed, the *SS* grew explosively, initially by recruiting in Germany, then by taking on German-speaking *Volksdeutscher* from the occupied territories, evolving into a kind of foreign legion manned by non-German troops from all over Europe, and ending the war as a million-strong force used to spearhead many of the *Wehrmacht*'s last offensives. Dedicated fanatics, they believed in the *Führer* and ultimate victory longer than any other group, but to no avail as the Third Reich came crashing down.

WAFFEN-SS RANKS AND THEIR ENGLISH EQUIVALENTS

SS-Schütze — Private

SS-Oberschütze — Senior Private, attained after six months' service

SS-Sturmmann — Lance-Corporal

SS-Rottenführer — Corporal

SS-Unterscharführer — Senior Corporal/Lance-Sergeant

SS-Scharführer — Sergeant

SS-Oberscharführer — Staff Sergeant

SS-Hauptscharführer — Warrant Officer

SS-Sturmscharführer — Senior Warrant Officer after 15 years' service

SS-Untersturmführer — Second Lieutenant

SS-Obersturmführer — First Lieutenant

SS-Hauptsturmführer — Captain

SS-Sturmbannführer — Major

SS-Oberbannsturmführer — Lieutenant-Colonel

SS-Standartenführer — Colonel

SS-Oberführer — Senior Colonel

SS-Brigadeführer und *Generalmajor der Waffen-SS* — Major-General

SS-Gruppenführer und *Generalleutnant der Waffen-SS* — Lieutenant-General

SS-Obergruppenführer und *General der Waffen-SS* — General

SS-Oberstgruppenführer und *Generaloberst der Waffen-SS* — Colonel-General

Reichsführer-SS — (no English equivalent)

INDEX